THE
WORLD
AND ITS
PEOPLE
A GEOGRAPHY SOURCE BOOK

CW01464368

BLITZ

The World and its People

A GRISEWOOD AND DEMPSEY BOOK

First published in 1992 by Blitz Editions,
an imprint of Bookmart Limited,
Registered Number 2372865.
Trading as Bookmart Limited,
Desford Road, Enderby,
Leicester, LE5 5AD.

10 9 8 7 6 5 4 3 2 1

The material in this book was previously
published by Grisewood & Dempsey Ltd.
in *Children's Illustrated Encyclopedia*
1990.

© Grisewood and Dempsey Ltd. 1990,
1992.

ISBN 1 856050 34 3

Printed and bound in Italy

CONTENTS

THE WORLD AND ITS PEOPLE   **6**

Land and Sea   **8**

Weather   **12**

Environment   **14**

Peoples   **18**

COUNTRIES   **28**

Africa   **30**

The Americas   **36**

Asia   **42**

Australasia   **48**

Europe   **52**

Polar Regions   **60**

FACTS AND FIGURES   **62**

INDEX   **92**

Beliefs   **20**

Sport   **22**

Laws and Government   **24**

Trade   **26**

THE WORLD AND ITS PEOPLE

LAND AND SEA

How are mountains and volcanoes made? What causes ocean currents and waves? The face of Earth is always changing, as the planet ages. (See page 8.)

WEATHER

The weather affects how people live, how plants and animals behave. How is weather made? Why does it rain? What are clouds? (See page 12.)

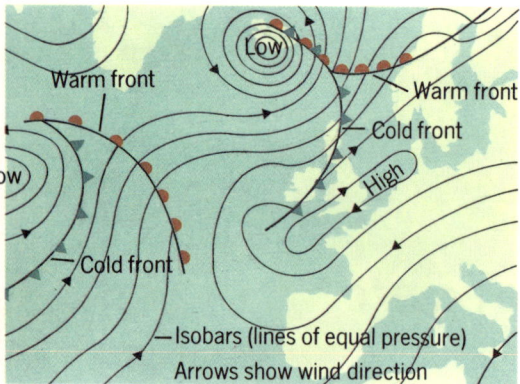

Warm front
Low
Warm front
Cold front
ow
High
Cold front
Isobars (lines of equal pressure)
Arrows show wind direction

ENVIRONMENT

Each of the Earth's environments has its own climate, vegetation and animal life. Looking after the environment is our responsibility. (See page 14.)

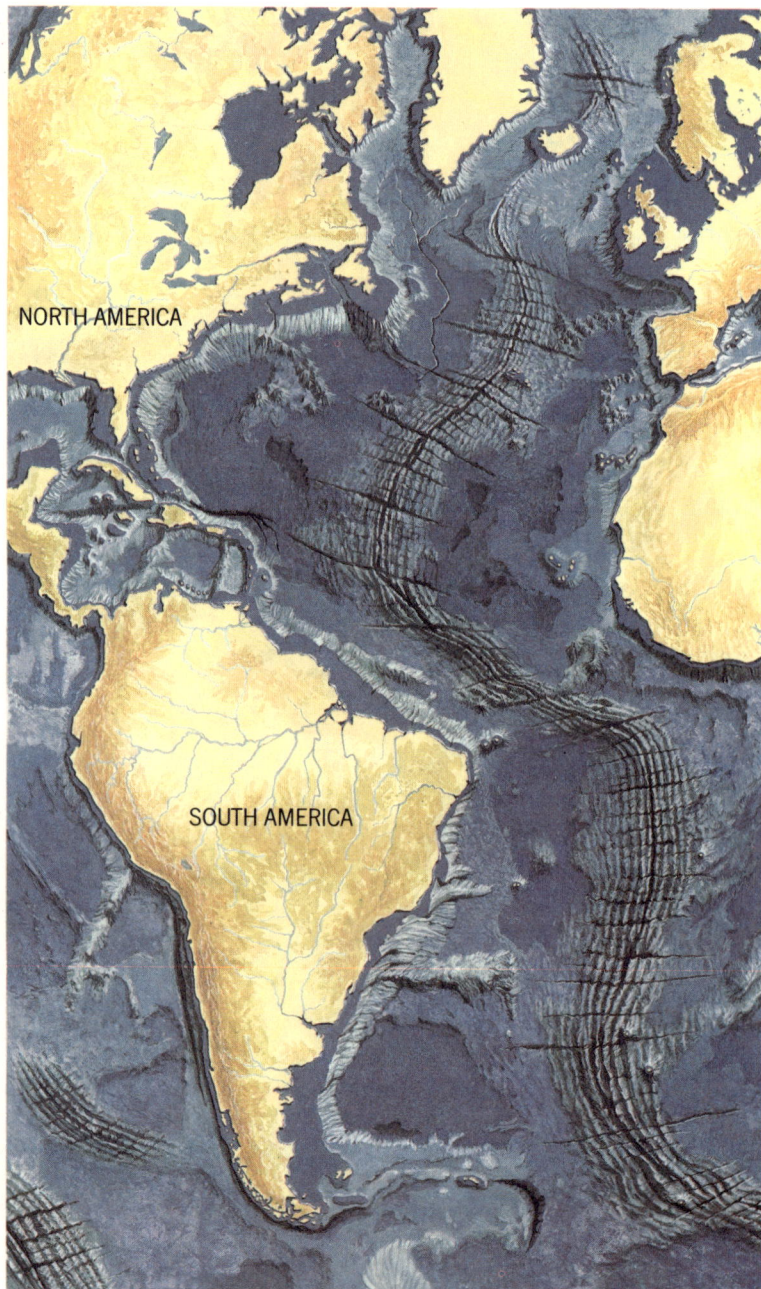

NORTH AMERICA

SOUTH AMERICA

PEOPLES
Humans are the most widespread species. There are more than five billion people on our planet. (See page 18.)

BELIEFS
Religious beliefs and many different customs have influenced human society. (See page 20.)

SPORT
In the past few people had time for leisure. Now sports and pastimes are enjoyed worldwide. (See page 22.)

LAWS AND GOVERNMENT
We live by laws. Who makes the laws, and how did governments and parliaments come about? (See page 24.)

TRADE
People in many countries earn their living making, buying and selling goods. The Industrial Revolution is still going on all over the world. (See page 26.)

1. Volcanic islands are shaped like cones.

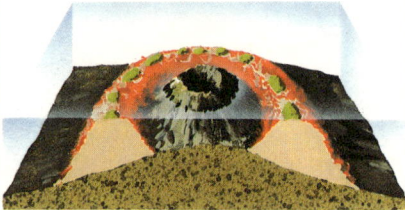

2. In time the volcanic island may sink below the water.

3. Only a coral reef, or atoll, remains above the water.

Below: Inside a volcano molten rock or magma is forced up through the Earth's crust. Cones of ash and lava (hot, liquid rock), domes or batholiths and geysers may result.

Land and Sea

Geologists and geophysicists, the scientists who study the Earth, believe that it is made of several layers. The crust or outer layer is comparatively thin. It is thicker beneath the continents, which are made of lighter rocks than the ocean floors. Beneath the crust is the mantle, which is probably slightly liquid and moves very slowly. This movement is gradually shifting the continents and the ocean floors. The evidence of this today is in earthquakes and volcanic eruptions. Geologists believe that millions of years ago the continents were joined together, and have drifted apart.

The core of the Earth is thought to be partly molten and partly solid. It is probably mainly made of iron and nickel. Like the mantle, the core is almost certainly moving – and its movement may make the Earth act like a magnet, causing a compass needle to point north.

Two hundred million years ago, all the continents lay jammed close together to form one mighty mass of land. Geographers call it Pangaea, meaning 'all Earth'. By 100 million years ago Pangaea had begun to break up as conti-

Key: 1 Volcanic cone. **2** Volcano's vent. **3** Magma. **4** Lava flow. Magma may penetrate the rock strata to form **5** a dyke, **6** a sill, **7** a batholith. **8** Extinct volcano. **9** Geyser.

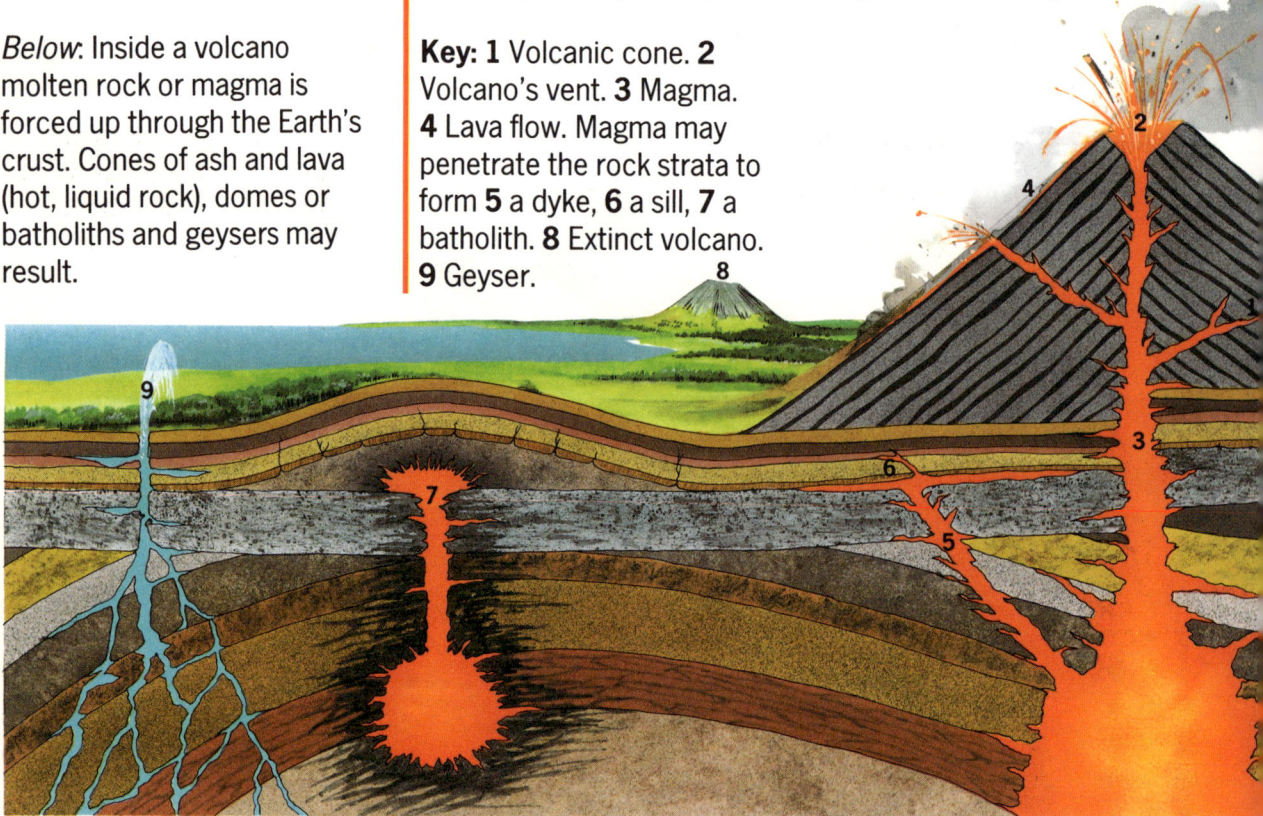

nents drifted apart. For a while there may have been two super-continents. North America, Europe and most of Asia formed one northern continent called Laurasia. South America, Africa, India, Antarctica and Australia formed a southern continent: Gondwanaland.

By 50 million years ago South America became a giant island. India was drifting north towards Asia. Today, a corridor of land joins North and South America. India has collided with Asia (pushing up the Himalayan mountains).

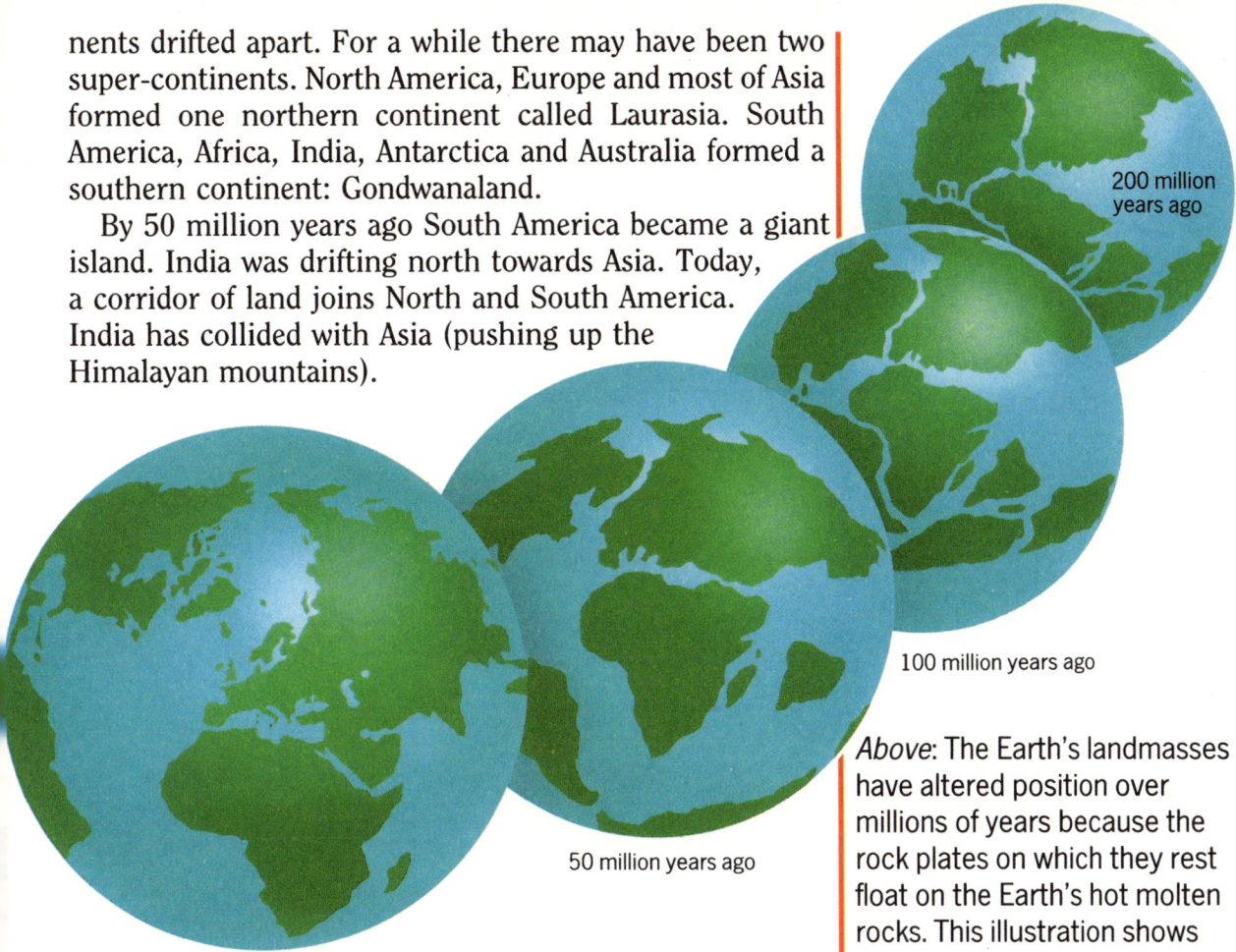

200 million years ago

100 million years ago

50 million years ago

Above: The Earth's landmasses have altered position over millions of years because the rock plates on which they rest float on the Earth's hot molten rocks. This illustration shows how the continents we know today have taken shape gradually over the past 200 million years.

Right: Caves are formed by the wearing away of rock by water. Caverns form in limestone because underground streams flow through the rock and slowly dissolve away the limestone. Stalactites and stalagmites form as water drips slowly from the cave roof, leaving tiny deposits of mineral behind. This section through a limestone cave system shows numerous caves and tunnels, with **1** stalactites, **2** a stalagmite, **3** a natural rock column, **4** a stream entering from the surface of the rock, **5** a stream re-emerging at the base of the limestone.

Right: Around the continents is an area of shallow water, called the continental shelf. It is about 180 metres (590 feet) deep. Beyond the shelf, the ocean floor slopes away into deeper water. It flattens out at about 3650 metres (11,975 feet). The bottom of the ocean is a flat plain, crossed by ridges and trenches. Rising from it are mountains and volcanoes. A bathyscaphe has descended 11,033 metres (36,198 feet) into the Mariana Trench in the Pacific Ocean.

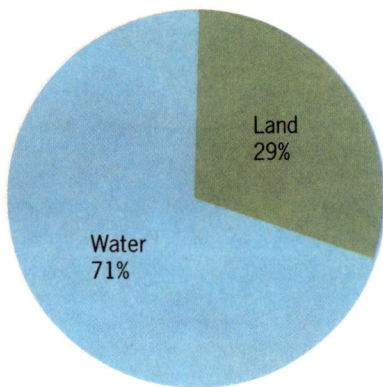

Above: Water covers 71 per cent of the Earth's surface.

Below: The chief minerals in sea water.

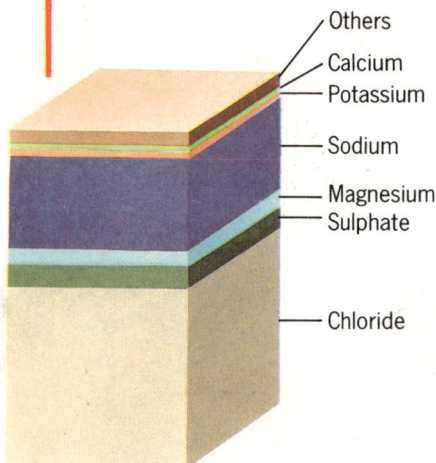

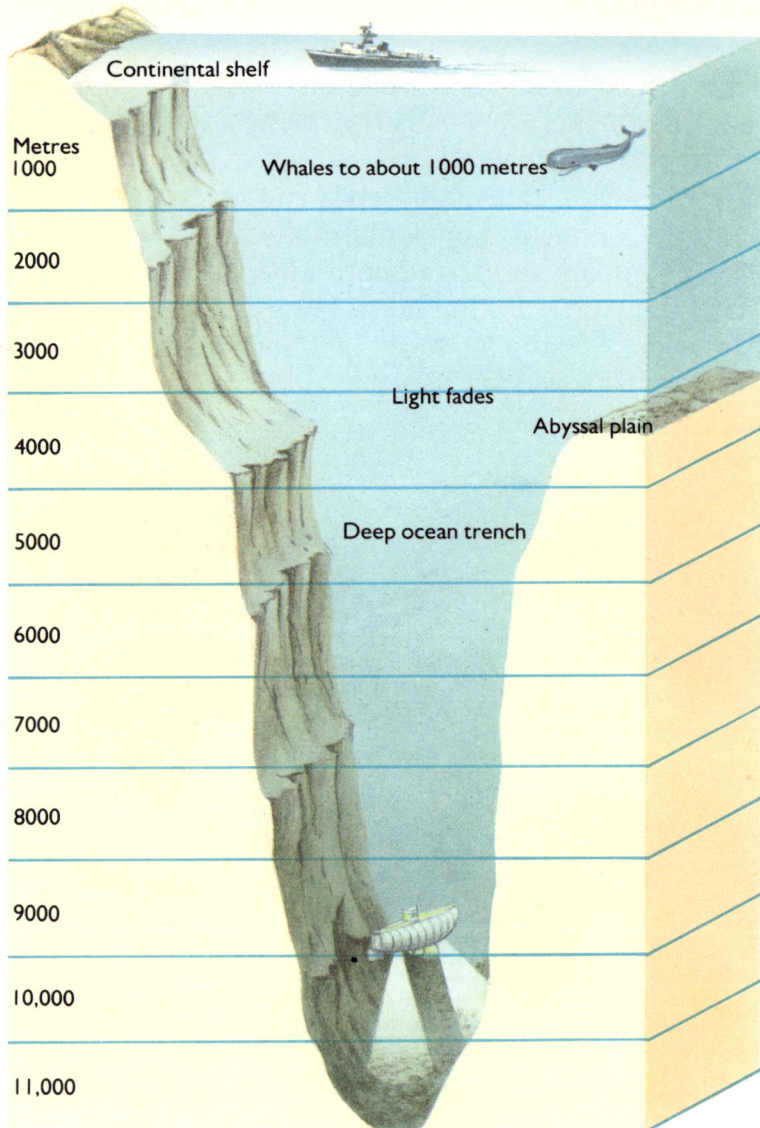

Almost three-quarters of the Earth's surface is covered by sea. Beneath the water is a landscape quite like that of the dry land. There are mountains and valleys, plateaus and plains. Around the edges of the great continents runs a sloping platform. The shallow water on this continental shelf is rich in plant and animal life.

The oceanic crust is made up of a series of curved plates, constantly grinding together to form ridges and trenches. The deepest parts of the sea lie in the Pacific Ocean. Here the crust disappears into trenches delving deep into the Earth's interior. The deepest of the ocean trenches is the Mariana Trench in the eastern Pacific Ocean. It is 11,033 metres (36,198 feet) deep. The deepest point in the Atlantic Ocean is 8,648 metres (28,373 feet) in the Puerto Rico Trench. Because of all this movement, the oldest rocks found on the seabed are only 200 million years old – much younger than rocks found on land.

OCEAN CURRENTS

North Pacific Drift

North Equatorial Current

Equatorial Counter Current

South Equatorial Current

Gulf Stream

North Atlantic Drift

Canaries Current

North Equatorial Current

Brazil Current

Benguela Current

West Wind Drift

West Wind Drift

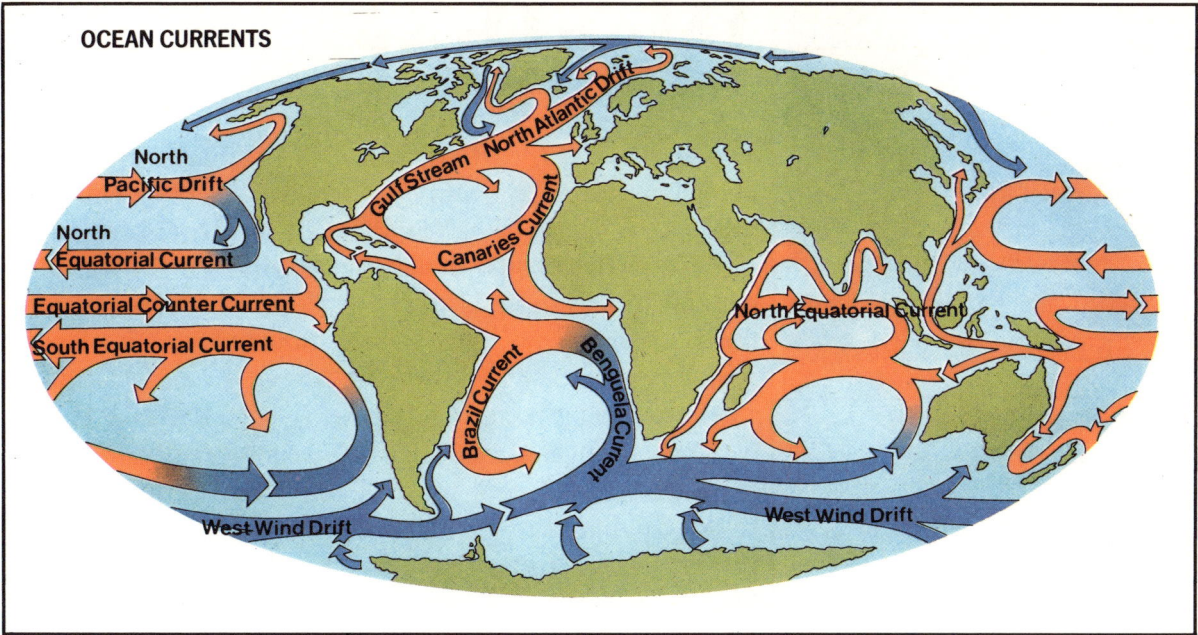

Ocean currents are caused by the movement of warm and cold water. Currents flow in regular patterns. The warm waters of the North Atlantic Drift, which flows from the Gulf of Mexico across the Atlantic, keep winters in Britain mild. The wind causes waves. A wave breaks when the water at its crest starts moving quicker than the rest of the wave, toppling over on itself. Wave action can erode, or wear away, the coastline.

Below: Although waves move, the water does not travel forwards, but circles.

Right: Spilling waves build up beaches, but plunging waves are destructive.

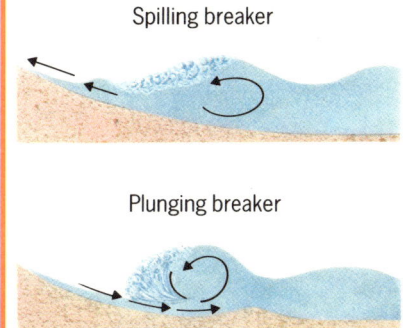

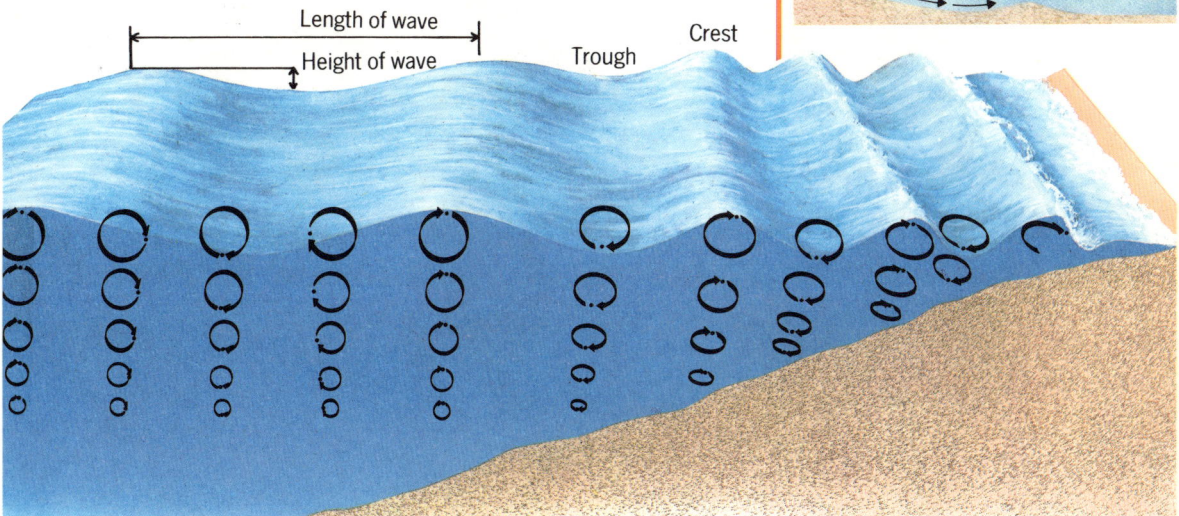

Above: A map showing the chief ocean currents. Red arrows indicate warm currents and blue arrows, cold currents.

Spilling breaker

Plunging breaker

Length of wave

Height of wave

Trough

Crest

11

Weather

The weather of a particular part of the Earth over a long period is called its climate. The weather at any place depends on conditions in the Earth's atmosphere. The most important cause of weather is wind. Hot air rises and cool air moves in underneath it. Huge masses of air, some hot and some cool, are always moving over the Earth's surface as wind.

At the Equator and at the North and South Poles the weather changes very little. It is hot most of the time at the Equator and cold most of the time at the Poles. Between the Equator and the Poles there are areas known as the temperate zones. Here the weather is generally mild but changes a good deal. Hot air and cold air are constantly meeting to form regions of low pressure called depressions, which bring unsettled weather.

Weather forecasters show what is happening on charts showing winds, temperatures and pressures. Weather ships at sea, balloons, and satellites in space collect information about the changing weather.

Above left: When storms have wind speeds over 120 kilometres per hour they are called hurricanes. This is the eye or centre of a hurricane.

Below: This map shows the amount of water falling in one year in different places. Most falls as rain, but some falls as hail, sleet or snow.

THE BEAUFORT SCALE

The Beaufort Scale is used to classify wind strength.

0	Smoke rises straight up
1	Smoke drifts gently
2	Wind felt on face
3	Leaves and twigs move
4	Small branches sway; dust blows
5	Small trees sway; waves break on lakes
6	Large branches move
7	Whole trees move; walking difficult
8	Twigs break off
9	Chimneys may be blown off houses
10	Trees are uprooted
11	Widespread damage
12	Violent destruction

WORLD RAINFALL

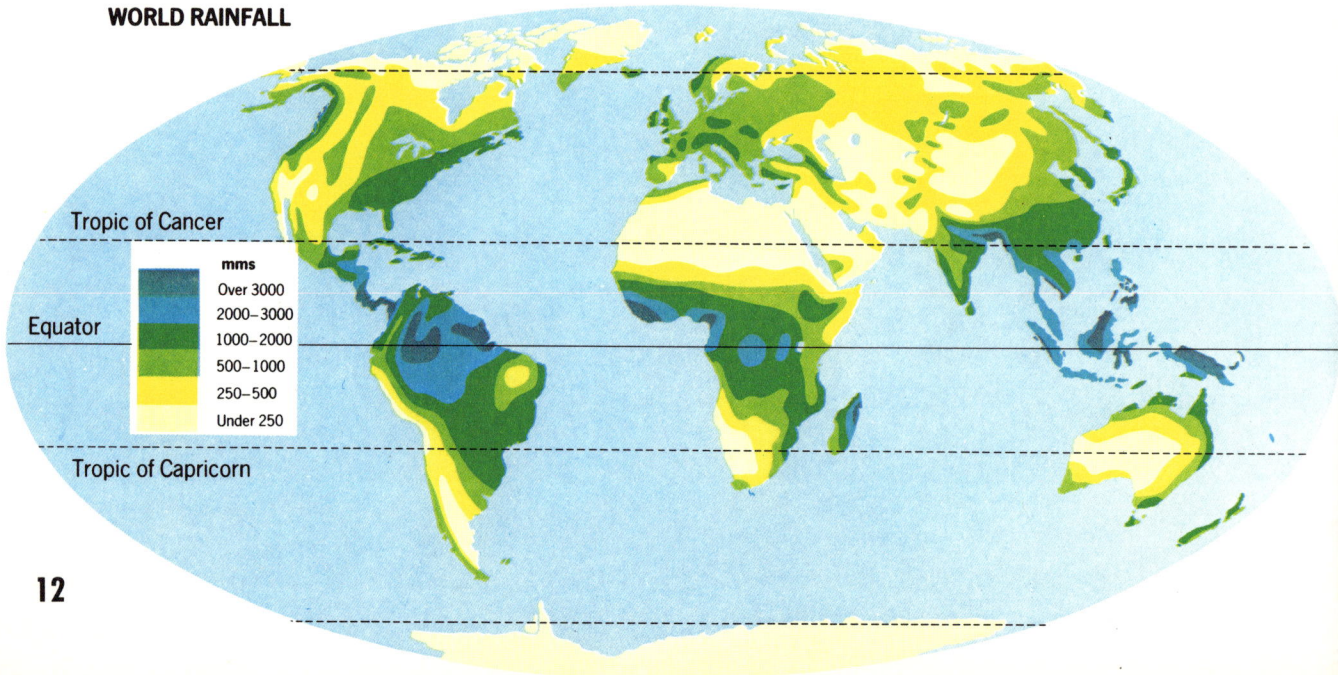

Tropic of Cancer

Equator

Tropic of Capricorn

mms
Over 3000
2000–3000
1000–2000
500–1000
250–500
Under 250

Cold air mass

Warm air mass

Cold air mass

Cold front

Warm Front

TYPES OF CLOUD

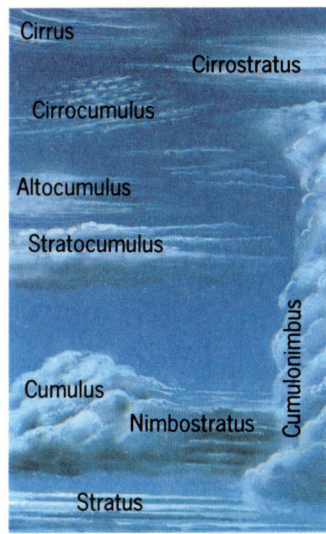

Cirrus
Cirrostratus
Cirrocumulus
Altocumulus
Stratocumulus
Cumulus
Nimbostratus
Cumulonimbus
Stratus

Cirrus: High, wispy ice clouds.
Cirrostratus: Milky, thin, high cloud producing a halo round the Sun.
Cirrocumulus: Thin high lines of cloud with rippled edges.
Altostratus: A greyish sheet of cloud with a hazy Sun above.
Altocumulus: Fleecy bands of cloud with blue sky between.
Stratocumulus: Like a low, dark heavy kind of altocumulus.
Cumulus: A white, heaped-up cloud usually seen in fair weather.
Nimbostratus: Low, grey, sheet-like cloud producing steady rain.
Stratus: Low grey sheet-like cloud.
Cumulonimbus: A towering cloud that may give heavy rain showers.

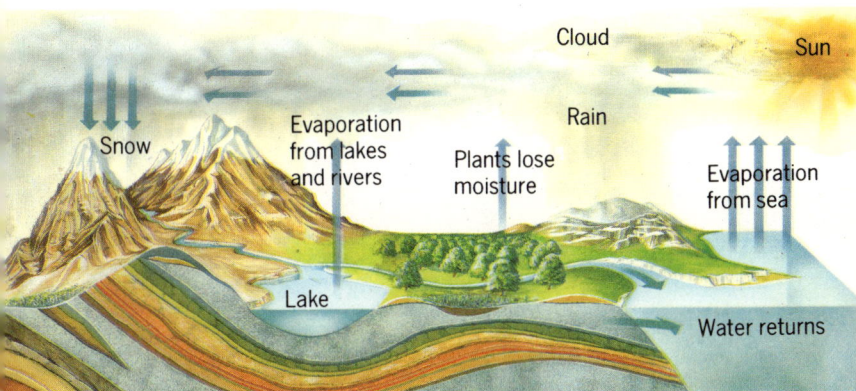

Above: A depression, or circling mass of low pressure, often brings rain at both the cold and warm fronts.

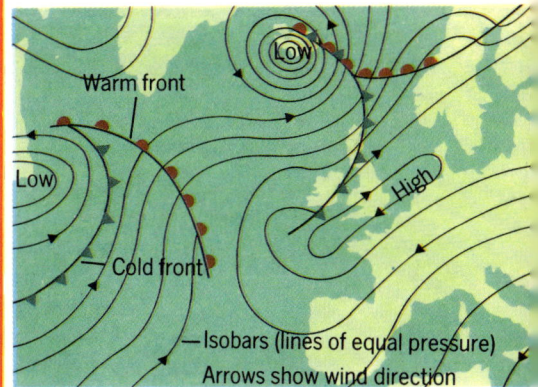

Low
Warm front
Low
High
Cold front
Isobars (lines of equal pressure)
Arrows show wind direction

Above: Weather maps show what conditions to expect.

Left: The water cycle. The Sun's heat evaporates sea water. Rising vapour cools and condenses into droplets that form clouds. Water falls as rain, snow, sleet or hail and runs into rivers or the soil. Both surface and underground water flows back to the sea.

Cloud
Sun
Rain
Snow
Evaporation from lakes and rivers
Plants lose moisture
Evaporation from sea
Lake
Water returns

13

Above: A huge sand dune. Sand dunes are shaped by the wind and, as their tops are blown, they move across the desert.

Above: A glacier is a river of ice moving very slowly down a mountainside.

Right: Savanna consists mainly of grassland with a few widely scattered trees such as acacia and baobab. Many savanna regions suffer periods of drought – in some regions for up to five months. A wide variety of animals has become adapted to these environmental conditions. Giraffes, for example, get most of their food and moisture from leaves, and can go for over a month without drinking.

Environment

Animal and plant communities live in particular habitats, or environments. These are classified according to vegetation, which in turn depends on the climate.

Some of the world's wettest areas are near the Equator. It is always hot. The natural vegetation is luxuriant rain forest, with tall trees and dangling creepers.

The world's driest places are hot deserts in the tropics, a zone either side of the Equator. Years may pass with little or no rain, but when storms do come, plants can spring up overnight from dormant seeds.

Between the rain forest and the deserts are areas where it rains only at certain times of the year. In Asia, heavy rain falls during the monsoon. In Africa and South America, the savanna vegetation is well suited to these climatic conditions. The savanna is mainly grass, dotted with trees that can withstand the long dry season.

Away from the tropics, the climate gets steadily colder towards the Poles. Near the tropical deserts it is still warm in the winter, as it is around the Mediterranean Sea. The centres of the continents, far from the coast, are dry and have very cold winters. In some parts the vegetation is true desert, other areas have grasslands which are sometimes called steppes or prairies. Places facing winds blowing from the oceans, such as the Atlantic coast of Western Europe, are milder and wetter. In this part of the world the natural vegetation is deciduous forest.

Vast areas of coniferous forest stretch across the cold

Above: Mexico has a wide variety of landscapes and climates within relatively short distances of one another: from mountains and plateaus, which cover two thirds of the land, to tropical forests, deserts and fertile valleys.

Left: In temperate climates, spring and summer are the main growing seasons.

northern lands. In the far north the vegetation is tundra – mosses, lichens and low plants which can survive the cold. It snows rather than rains, but there is plenty of water in the summer when the snow melts. Near the Arctic and Antarctic Poles, permanent snow and ice take over. There is hardly any vegetation, and few animals can survive the harsh conditions.

Below: A tropical rain forest has four main levels. Shrubs, climbing plants and mosses cover the forest floor above which grow small trees and seedlings. Above, a mass of touching tree tops forms a dense canopy, shutting out sunlight. The tallest trees break through the canopy in places to form the top layer.

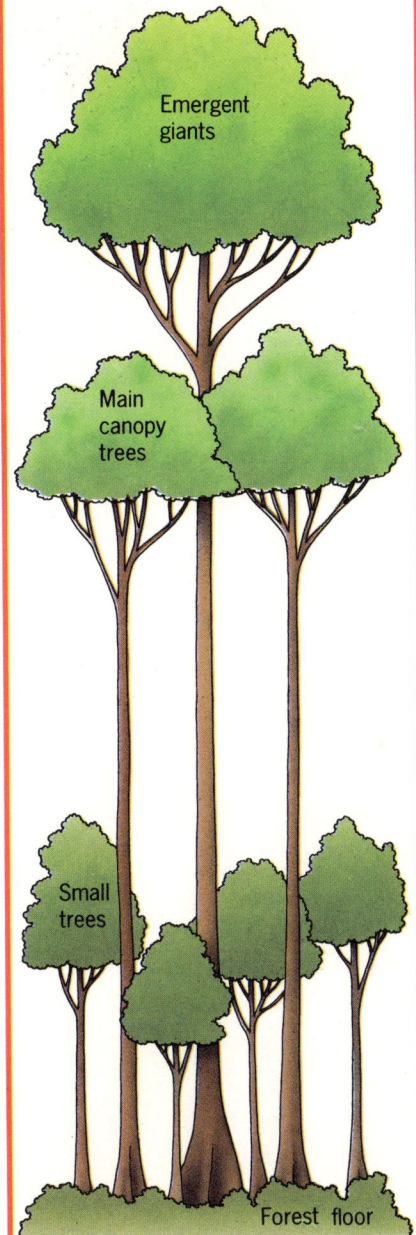

Emergent giants

Main canopy trees

Small trees

Forest floor

Below: All over the world, endangered animals and plants will face extinction unless more is done to protect them. This map shows just some of the animal species that are in danger.

The Earth is constantly changing. Underground forces can shift continents, raise mountains, and cause earthquakes and volcanic eruptions. Waves, winds, rivers and rainfall alter the surface shape of the land. This is a natural change to the environment.

Human beings too can alter the Earth's environment. Humans have cut down much of the natural forest that once covered vast areas. Huge tracts of rain forest are

Spanish lynx

Polar Bear

Wood bison

Walrus (killed for ivory)

Pyreneean ibex

American alligator

Mexican grizzly bear

Caribbean monk seal

3

Jenink's duiker

4

● Most threatened protected areas

United Nations Environmental Programme

1.   Mediterranean Region
2.   Kuwait Action Plan Region
3.   Caribbean Region
4.   West and Central African Region
5.   East African Region
6/7. Red Sea and Gulf of Aden Region
8.   South West Pacific Region
9.   South East Pacific Region
10. South West Altantic Region

Manatee

Hyacinth macaw (illegal export)

Woolly spider monkey

9

Maned wolf

10

Mountain zebra

Juan Fernandez fur seal

Blue whale

being felled each year, both for timber and to make room for ranchers and farmers. Without the trees, the soil quickly becomes infertile and barren. Chemical pollution from our factories and cities fouls the air, the soil, and the rivers and lakes. Wildlife loses its habitat and many species face extinction. These problems must be tackled and solved if we are to protect the planet. Looking after the environment is something we must all do.

Reindeer (threatened by nuclear fallout)

Wolf

Siberian crane

Siberian tiger

European bison

Imperial eagle

Markhor

Przewalski's horse

Bald ibis

1

Pygmy hog

Persian fallow deer

2

Giant panda

Arabian oryx

6

Giant rafflesai (world's largest plant)

Kouprey wild ox

Rhino (illegal export)

7

Addax

Sumatran rhino

Green turtle

Mountain gorilla

8

Black lechwe

Indri

5

White-throated wallaby

Noisy scrub bird

Southern sea otter

Humpback whale

Below: People speak many different languages and dialects (local versions of a language). The most widely spoken languages belong to a group called Indo-European. The diagram shows how these languages are grouped in related families, even though they sound different. Indo-European languages originated in Europe, central and southwest Asia, and India. They include English (the world's most widely spoken language) which belongs to the Germanic group. The Romance languages include French, Spanish, Portuguese and Italian. Russian belongs to the Balto-Slavic group; Bengali to the Indo-Iranian group. Chinese, which is spoken by a fifth of the world's people, belongs to a separate family.

Peoples

There are more than 5000 million people in the world. This means that there are only about 30 people to every square kilometre of land. But 20 per cent of the Earth's surface is too dry to support many people; another 20 per cent is too cold; 20 per cent is too rugged and mountainous; and nearly 20 per cent is dense tropical forest. That leaves only 20 per cent of the Earth's surface to support the vast majority of the world's people.

There are three main racial groups making up the Earth's people. They are known as the Caucasoid, Negroid and Mongoloid groups. These people speak an amazing number of languages and dialects, which are related to each other in language families.

Through most of history the world's population has increased steadily but slowly. Population increases when there are more births than deaths. In the last 200 years, the population of the world has leapt from 800 million to over 5000 million. This is because medical science has been able to conquer many killer diseases, such as smallpox, tuberculosis and cholera. So, although parents are actually producing fewer babies now than in the past, more

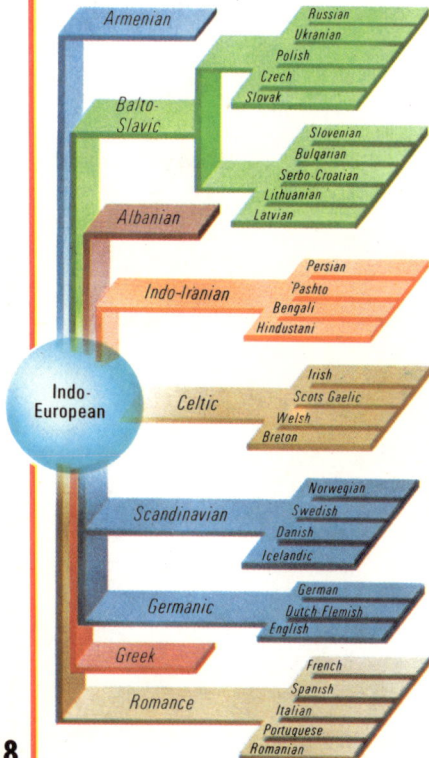

European

Indian

Aborigine

Arabic

Chinese

North American Indian

Negroid

Caribbean

Left, *below left*: We all belong to one species, *Homo sapiens*. However, scientists divide humankind into Caucasoids, Mongoloids and Negroids. The Caucasoid peoples include Europeans, Iranians, Afghans, northern and eastern Africans, and most of the peoples of India. Australian Aboriginals are also Caucasoids. The Chinese are Mongoloid people. So are the Japanese and the Koreans, and the Indians of North and South America. Negroid people include the Papuans of New Guinea, Negritos of Australasia, and certain groups of African people.

Below: The bar chart shows how the populations of developed and developing countries have increased between 1750 and 1975, and estimates the population for the year 2000. The pie chart (inset) gives the percentage of the world's population in each of the largest countries.

of them live to grow up and have children of their own.

The populations of Africa, Asia, and Central and South America are increasing rapidly. Many countries in these continents have a 'young' population, with nearly half of their people under 15 years of age. The growth of population is much slower in the richer developed nations of North America, Europe, Russia and the former Republics of the USSR and most of Australasia. In these nations, people have smaller families and the trend is for the population to become 'older'.

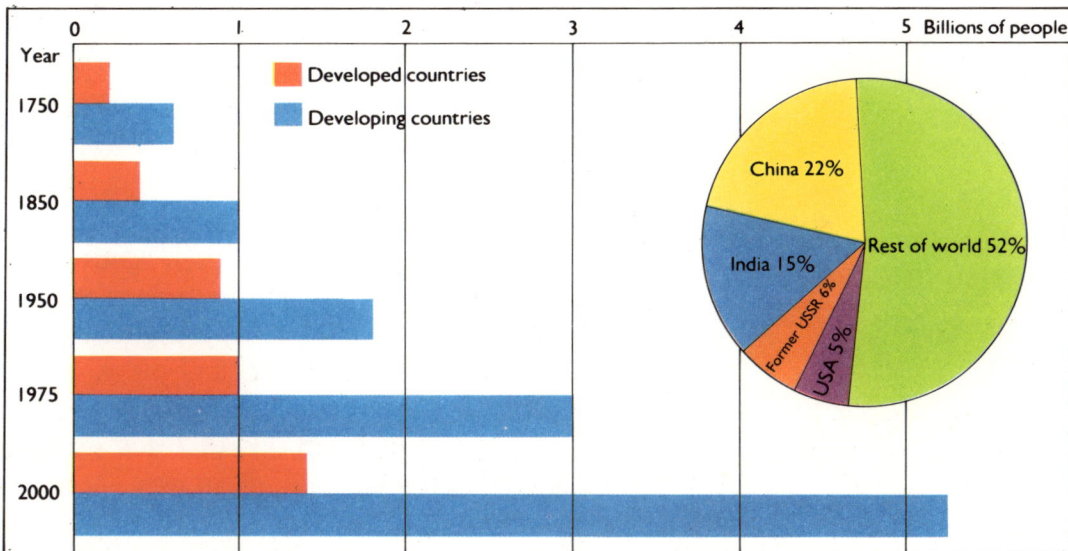

Bar chart: Billions of people (0 to 5)

Developed countries
Developing countries

Years: 1750, 1850, 1950, 1975, 2000

Pie chart:
- China 22%
- Rest of world 52%
- India 15%
- Former USSR 6%
- USA 5%

Above: The Sphinx and the Pyramids of Egypt were built by a people who believed in many gods. The Egyptians buried their kings in huge tombs, along with treasure, and other worldly possessions they thought necessary for the afterlife.

Below: The Hindu god Ganesh, son of Shiva and Parvati, is the teacher and the remover of obstacles. Hindus pray to Ganesh before major projects, as he is thought to bring success.

Beliefs

Since earliest times, people have believed in gods or spirits from another world. Many customs and ways of life developed as a result of these beliefs. The peoples of the ancient world – the Egyptians, Greeks and Romans for instance – had complex religious beliefs, with many gods.

All the world's great religions began in Asia. The oldest religion to teach that there is only one God is Judaism, the religion of the Jews. Its history is told in the Hebrew Bible, which Christians call the Old Testament. Islam was founded by the prophet Muhammad. Its followers are called Muslims. They believe in Allah, the one God. Muslims pray in a mosque and obey the teachings of the Koran, their holy book.

Hinduism is the chief religion of India. Hindus believe people's souls are reborn many times until good enough to join Brahman, a supreme power. Their gods include Vishnu and Shiva. Buddhism is another important Eastern religion. Its founder, the Buddha ('The Enlightened One'), taught that people have many lives, and move gradually towards perfection and peace.

People who follow the teachings of Jesus Christ are Christians. Not all Christians belong to one Church, but most share certain basic beliefs; they believe that God

Left: A mosque is the place of worship for Muslims, followers of the religion of Islam. From the tall minarets, the muezzins call the faithful to prayers. This mosque, Hagia Sophia, is in Istanbul in Turkey where many people are Muslims.

Below: Statues of Buddha are found in temples throughout Asia, where Buddhism thrives. Here, he is portrayed in a characteristic pose with his legs folded. The Buddha was Siddhartha Gautama. He was born about 563 BC in northern India and was the founder of Buddhism.

made the world, that Jesus was His Son and that through faith in His death and resurrection people can be forgiven their sins and can gain eternal life.

Other important world religions are Confucianism, Taoism, Zoroastrianism, Shintoism and Sikhism.

People who believe in no god and have no religion are called atheists. An agnostic is someone who does not know whether or not there is a god.

Above: A Jewish boy studies the scriptures for the bar mitzvah ceremony. The most important sacred books of Judaism are the Torah and Talmud.

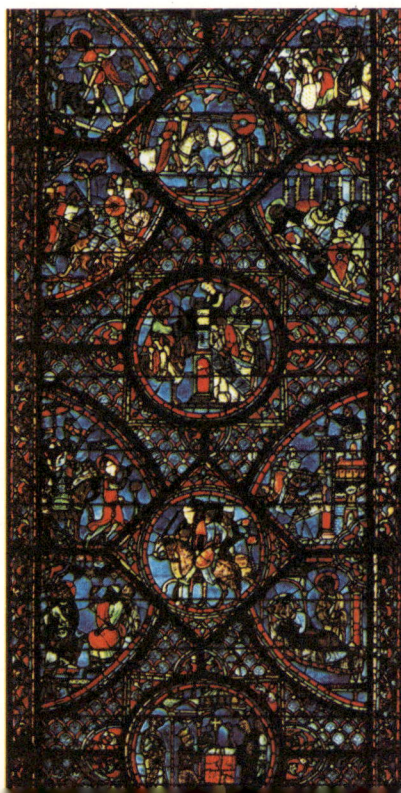

Left: Christian churches often have beautiful stained glass windows with illustrations from Bible stories and the lives of the saints. This window is found in the 13th-century cathedral at Chartres, France. Churches with elaborate decoration are built to glorify God, and as places in which Christians can worship Him together.

21

Above: Competitors from many nations gather every four years for the Olympic Games.

Below: A downhill skier. Skiers also compete in jumping and cross-country races.

Right: Gymnasts performing on the rings and the bar. Both exercises call for strength and timing.

Sport

People enjoy many recreations – games as different as chess and football; outdoor activities such as sailing, riding, climbing and walking; indoor leisure pursuits such as squash, table tennis, judo or country dancing.

Today, people have more leisure time than ever before. To keep healthy and active, your body needs exercise. Taking part in sport is an excellent way of keeping fit, meeting new friends and having fun. People are most active between adolescence and around the age of 30. Our bodies

Above: A cricket bat, wicket (stumps with bails on top), pads and a ball. Cricket began in England in the 1700s.

Above left: American 'gridiron' football is now watched and played in other countries as well as in the USA.

are then at their strongest. However, many people continue to enjoy sports and hobbies into old age.

Organized sport has a long history. The Olympic Games were first held in Greece in 776 BC. Competitors took part in sports such as athletics, boxing and wrestling, and also in poetry and arts competitions. The modern Olympic Games, inspired by those of Ancient Greece, were begun in 1896 and are held every four years. Thousands of athletes gather to take part in a variety of sports. There are separate Games for winter sports, such as skiing and skating. Several sports (archery, for example) began as military exercises for soldiers. The popular games of today such as soccer, tennis, baseball and rugby were 'organized' in the 19th century. Ruling bodies were formed, and the laws of each sport were clearly drawn up. In the 20th century contests have become international, and spectator sport has become both an entertainment and a business.

Sumo wrestling

Judo

Above: Fencing developed from sword-fighting and military training.

Left: Sumo wrestlers *(far left)* are giants, but bouts are soon over. Martial arts such as judo require lengthy training to perfect the various moves.

23

Above: Martin Luther King Jr led black Americans in the struggle for civil rights. He was murdered in 1968.

Below: England's King John agreeing to Magna Carta in 1215. The document stated that the people, as well as the king, had rights.

Laws and Government

Laws, or rules, and government (a system for making laws) were needed as soon as people began living in groups. In a primitive tribe the best hunter or strongest warrior might become the ruler or chief. At first the ruler was chosen by the members of the tribe. But then it became the custom that the ruler's son always took his place. This is known as 'hereditary rule'.

To help make sensible laws, good kings took advice from councils of wise people. In time, these councils grew almost as powerful as the king. The Ancient Greeks were the first to try a form of government called democracy or 'rule by the people'. The people met to discuss new laws and to decide what taxes should be paid. This was the beginning of the modern parliament.

Democracy took a long time to grow, and until the 1600s monarchs (kings and queens) remained powerful. A

challenge to their power came when the English parliament fought a war against the king. After this Civil War (1642–49), the English king or queen had to rule according to the laws of Parliament. When the Americans broke away from British rule (1776), they chose to be a republic. The US head of state is not a king, but an elected president. Most countries today are republics. In some republics, the president has a great deal of power. In others, the presidency is more ceremonial. Power lies with the government, headed by a prime minister.

In a democracy, people vote in elections to choose the law-makers. As well as voting for the country's government, we also vote in local government elections.

Above: The trial of King Charles I in 1649. Parliament challenged the king's right to rule without its consent, and this led to the Civil War. Charles was executed. His son eventually regained the throne, but power had shifted permanently away from the monarch and into the hands of Parliament.

Left: A law court in America. A country's laws are enforced by the courts, where cases are decided by a judge and jury.

25

Above: British ships in China in 1835. By the 19th century world trade was flourishing.

Above: Advertising seeks to increase public awareness about a product or company.

Trade

In ancient times and in the Middle Ages there was some trade between different parts of the world. Chinese silks and porcelain, precious stones from India and spices from South-East Asia reached Europe, but trade was in luxury goods only and on a small scale. After the discovery of North and South America, and the setting up of colonies there, precious metals came to Europe from Mexico and Peru. Spices and other goods were brought from Asia. Gold and silver helped the growth of international trade, linking Asia, America, Europe and Africa. A world economy was beginning to take shape.

The Industrial Revolution of the 1700s and 1800s gave another boost to world trade. Factories in western Europe could not get enough local raw materials and so traders went looking for them throughout the world. Britain imported raw cotton for the mills of Lancashire from the United States and Egypt. Tin for the plating and canning industries, and rubber for the transport and chemical industries were brought from Malaya. Australia and Canada became producers of wool, grain, timber and fruit.

Japan and West Germany rebuilt their industries after World War II with astonishing speed. By 1958 West Germany had overtaken Britain as an exporter of manufactured goods. Japan became the leading producer of electronic goods, and also a major exporter of cars and machinery. Other Asian nations, such as Taiwan and

Two different forms of trade – (*left*) bartering for goods at a street market, (*above*) trade on the stock exchange using sophisticated technology.

Below: An oil refinery. Oil is the world's most important fuel. Countries which have oil have become rich by selling it to countries which need oil for their industries. A rise in the price of oil can affect people in countries all over the world, putting up the prices of goods in the shops.

South Korea, have become important manufacturing centres, while China and India are fast building up their own industries. The countries of Eastern Europe have turned recently from rigid, state control of industry towards a free 'market economy'.

The effects of the Industrial Revolution and of the Technology Revolution of the 20th century are rapidly creating a world civilization. Different ways of life, customs and dress are becoming fewer. Many Asian and African teenagers wear jeans, watch television and listen to pop music just like young people in Europe and the United States.

COUNTRIES

AFRICA

Africa is the second largest continent and has the fastest-growing population in the world. (See page 30.)

THE AMERICAS

The Americas are made up of North America (including Central America and the West Indies) and South America. (See page 36.)

ASIA

Asia is the world's largest continent and has more people (over 2500 million) than any other continent. (See page 42.)

AUSTRALASIA

Australasia consists of Australia, New Zealand and many islands in the Pacific Ocean. (See page 48.)

EUROPE

Europe is the sixth largest continent, but the most densely populated. Only Asia, which is four times bigger, has more people. (See page 52.)

POLAR REGIONS

The Polar Regions of the Arctic and the Antarctic are cold and desolate and hardly anyone lives there. (See page 60.)

Below: A multicoloured display of national flags. Flags are symbols which stand for a country's people, land and its government.

INTERNATIONAL TIME ZONES

(Time zone map with hours marked: 1 2 3 4 5 6 7 8 9 10 11 12 am / pm 1 2 3 4 5 6 7 8 9 10 11 12 1 am, labelled Greenwich Meridian and International Date Line)

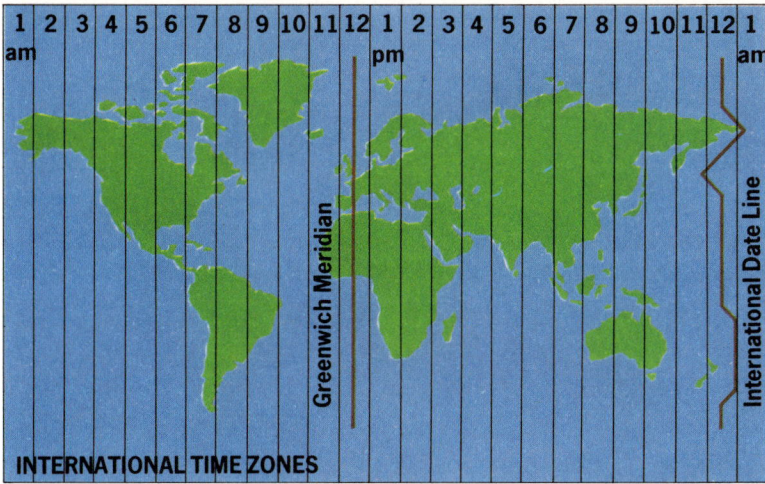

Left: Because the Earth rotates through 360° in 24 hours, there is one hour's time difference for every 15° of longitude. When it is midday in London (0°), it is 6 pm in the evening in Calcutta (90°E), but it is only sunrise and 6 am in Chicago (90°W). Each Time Zone covers about 15° of longitude, but the boundaries follow national or state borders.

Newspaper reports often divide the world into East and West. 'The East' usually refers to the Communist countries – which since the 1940s have been chiefly those of Eastern Europe, Russia and the former Republics of the USSR and China. The 'West' refers to Western Europe, USA, Canada, Australia and their allies.

Equally important is the 'North-South' divide. In the north are the developed countries of the world. Most of the rest of the world, south of the equator, is poor. Most southern countries are still struggling to develop. Some have huge debts, owed to foreign banks. Poverty, disease and hunger are serious problems. These developing countries are sometimes referred to as the Third World. Most of Central and South America, Africa and southern Asia belongs to the Third World.

Below: Lines of latitude and longitude on maps and globes are labelled in degrees. This is because they are measured by using angles at the centre of the Earth. 1° (degree) is divided into 60' (minutes). The lines drawn parallel to the Equator are called lines of latitude. The Equator is 0°, and latitude is measured North and South of the Equator. Lines of longitude are drawn from Pole to Pole.

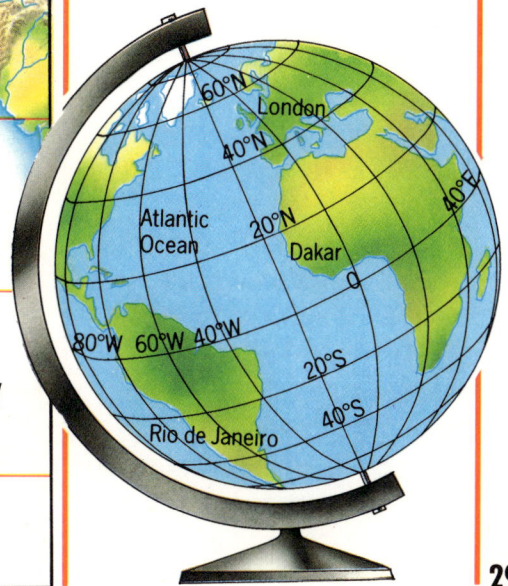

(Map of Africa showing: MEDITERRANEAN SEA, Atlas Mts, Sahara Desert, Nile, ASIA, Tropic of Cancer, Tibesti Mts, RED SEA, Niger, AFRICA, Great Rift Valley, Ethiopian Highlands, Equator, Zaire, Lake Victoria, SOUTH AMERICA, ATLANTIC OCEAN, Namib Desert, Zambezi, Kalahari Desert, INDIAN OCEAN, Tropic of Capricorn, Drakensberg)

(Globe showing: 60°N, London, 40°N, Atlantic Ocean, 20°N, Dakar, 40°E, 0, 80°W, 60°W, 40°W, 20°S, Rio de Janeiro, 40°S)

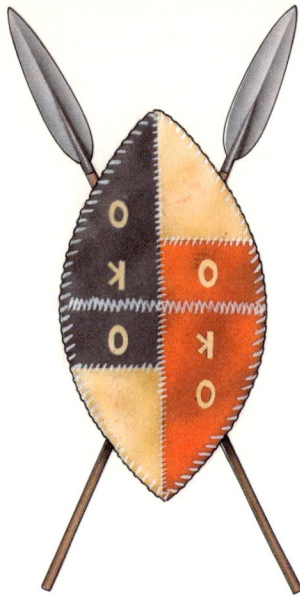

Above: Traditional shield and spears of the Masai, a nomadic group in Kenya. The Masai people are cattle herders and are well known for their skills in the use of weapons. More powerful in the 19th century, the Masai were weakened by the political changes and new diseases brought by the British colonists.

The symbol of the shield and spears is used in Kenya's national flag to represent the defence of freedom.

Right: European explorers such as Burton, Speke, Livingstone and Stanley journeyed across Africa in the 1800s. Livingstone made several expeditions into the African interior where he learned much about African customs, geography and the slave trade. His discoveries led to great competition among European nations for control of Africa.

Africa

Most of Africa is in the Tropics, but there are great differences in climate and vegetation. In North Africa there are mountains and a huge expanse of sand and rock called the Sahara Desert. It is hot and dry, with only scattered waterholes or oases. The equator runs through Central Africa. Here are hot and wet lowlands. There are thick rain forests, where the trees blot out the sunlight.

Elsewhere in Africa there are high rolling plains called *savannas*. It is cooler on the plains, but in the dry season no rain falls for months. When the rains come, plants grow very quickly. In the east are Africa's highest mountains: Kilimanjaro, which is 5895 metres above sea level, and Mount Kenya, which is 5200 metres above sea level.

Africa has some of the oldest rocks in the world, going back 3000 million years. In East Africa is a great crack, or fault, in the Earth's crust called the Great Rift Valley. In this area are Africa's largest lakes, Victoria, Nyasa and Tanganyika. Some of the world's longest rivers are in Africa. Longest of all is the Nile, followed by the Zaïre (Congo), the Niger and the Zambezi.

On the high plains of Africa lives a great variety of wild animals. Many have been killed by hunters and poachers. However, in game reserves visitors can see various kinds of antelopes, giraffes, zebras, elephants, leopards, lions and many other animals.

Much of Africa is thinly populated. The Sahara and other desert regions have no people at all. The tropical forests and grasslands are also thinly populated. Parts of

30

Nigeria are very densely populated and the Nile River valley is one of the world's most heavily populated regions. In the north of Africa the people are mainly Muslim Arabs or Berbers. South of the Sahara most of the people are black Africans. They are Christians or follow their own religions.

Below: There are 52 countries in Africa today. Sudan is the largest country with an area of 2,506,000 sq km (968,000 sq miles).

ATLANTIC OCEAN

MEDITERRANEAN SEA

Tangier
Algiers
Tunis
Constantine
TUNISIA
Rabat
Fés
Casablanca
Sfax
Tripoli
Benghazi
Marrakech
MOROCCO
ATLAS MOUNTAINS
Alexandria
Cairo
Suez

CANARY IS.

Las Palmas

WESTERN SAHARA

ALGERIA
SAHARA DESERT
LIBYA
EGYPT
Nile
Aswan

RED SEA

MAURITANIA
MALI
NIGER
CHAD
SUDAN
Dongola
Khartoum

Nouakchott
Senegal
Timbuktu
Agadez
L. Chad

Dakar
SENEGAL
Bamako
Niamey
N'Djamena
ETHIOPIA
Djibouti
Banjul
GAMBIA
BURKINA FASO
Ouagadougou
Kano
GUINEA BISSAU
Bissau
GUINEA
TOGO
BENIN
NIGERIA
Addis Ababa
Conakry
SIERRA LEONE
GHANA
Niger
Ibadan
CENTRAL AFRICAN REPUBLIC
ETHIOPIAN HIGHLANDS
Freetown
CÔTE D'IVOIRE
Lagos
Monrovia
Accra
Lomé
Porto-Novo
CAMEROON
SOMALI REPUBLIC
LIBERIA
Abidjan
Malabo
Yaoundé
Bangui
Mogadishu

SAO TOME & PRINCIPE
EQUATORIAL GUINEA
UGANDA
KENYA
Libreville
Kampala
Nairobi
M. Kenya
ATLANTIC OCEAN
GABON
CONGO
Zaire
CONGO BASIN
RWANDA
L. Victoria
Mombasa
Bujumbura
Kigali
M.
Kilimanjaro
■ Capital Cities
Brazzaville
BURUNDI
Zanzibar
Kinshasa
ZAIRE
Tabora
Dar es Salaam

0   500   1000 miles
0   500   1000   1500 Kilometres

Cabinda
L. Tanganyika
TANZANIA

Luanda
L. Malawi
COMORO IS.

ANGOLA
ZAMBIA
MALAWI
Benguela
Huambo
Lilongwe
MOZAMBIQUE
Antananarivo
Lusaka
Zambezi
MADAGASCAR

Harare
Beira

NAMIBIA
ZIMBABWE
Windhoek
BOTSWANA
Limpopo
Walvis Bay
KALAHARI DESERT
Gaborone
NAMIB DESERT
Pretoria
Maputo
Johannesburg
Mbabane
SWAZILAND
Orange
Maseru
Durban
SOUTH AFRICA
LESOTHO
Cape Town
DRAKENSBERG
East London
Port Elizabeth

INDIAN OCEAN

31

Right: Hungry children in a relief camp. Parts of Africa, such as Ethiopia, have been ravaged by famine. Some countries are torn by civil war; in others crops fail because of drought. Severe drought has been the cause of famine in Ethiopia several times in recent years. International aid has helped some of the starving, but many have died.

Below: The face of Africa is changing as modern cities grow larger and more crowded. Thirty per cent of Africans now live in towns. Cities with tall buildings, busy traffic and a network of roads can be found in virtually every African country.

They belong to many different tribes and speak many different languages. In Nigeria, in West Africa, there are about 250 languages. English, French and Portuguese are widely spoken. There are small groups of Bushmen and Pygmies, and people of Asian and European descent.

Most Africans are farmers. To feed themselves they grow crops of maize, yams, sweet potatoes, beans and fruit. Large farms called plantations grow crops such as cocoa-beans, coffee, oil palm, tea, tobacco, cotton and sugar.

Africa is rich in minerals. It produces gold, diamonds,

Algeria

Egypt

Ethiopia

Libya

Chad

Mauritania

Niger

Sudan

Morocco

Mali

Tunisia

Guinea

Benin

Cameroon

Cote d'Ivoire

Liberia

Congo

Gabon

Nigeria

Senegal

Gambia

Ghana

Sierra Leone

Togo

Burkina Faso

Burundi

CAR

Djibouti

Kenya

Rwanda

Tanzania

Uganda

Zaire

Mozambique

South Africa

Swaziland

Zambia

Zimbabwe

Angola

Botswana

Lesotho

Madagascar

Malawi

Above: A French mission station in Chad. By 1900, much of western Africa had come under French rule.

Below: In the 19th century each of the European powers established colonies for itself in Africa. Only Ethiopia managed to remain independent.

THE PARTITION OF AFRICA

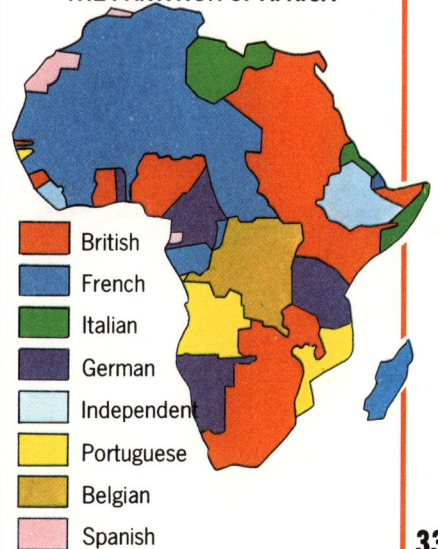

British
French
Italian
German
Independent
Portuguese
Belgian
Spanish

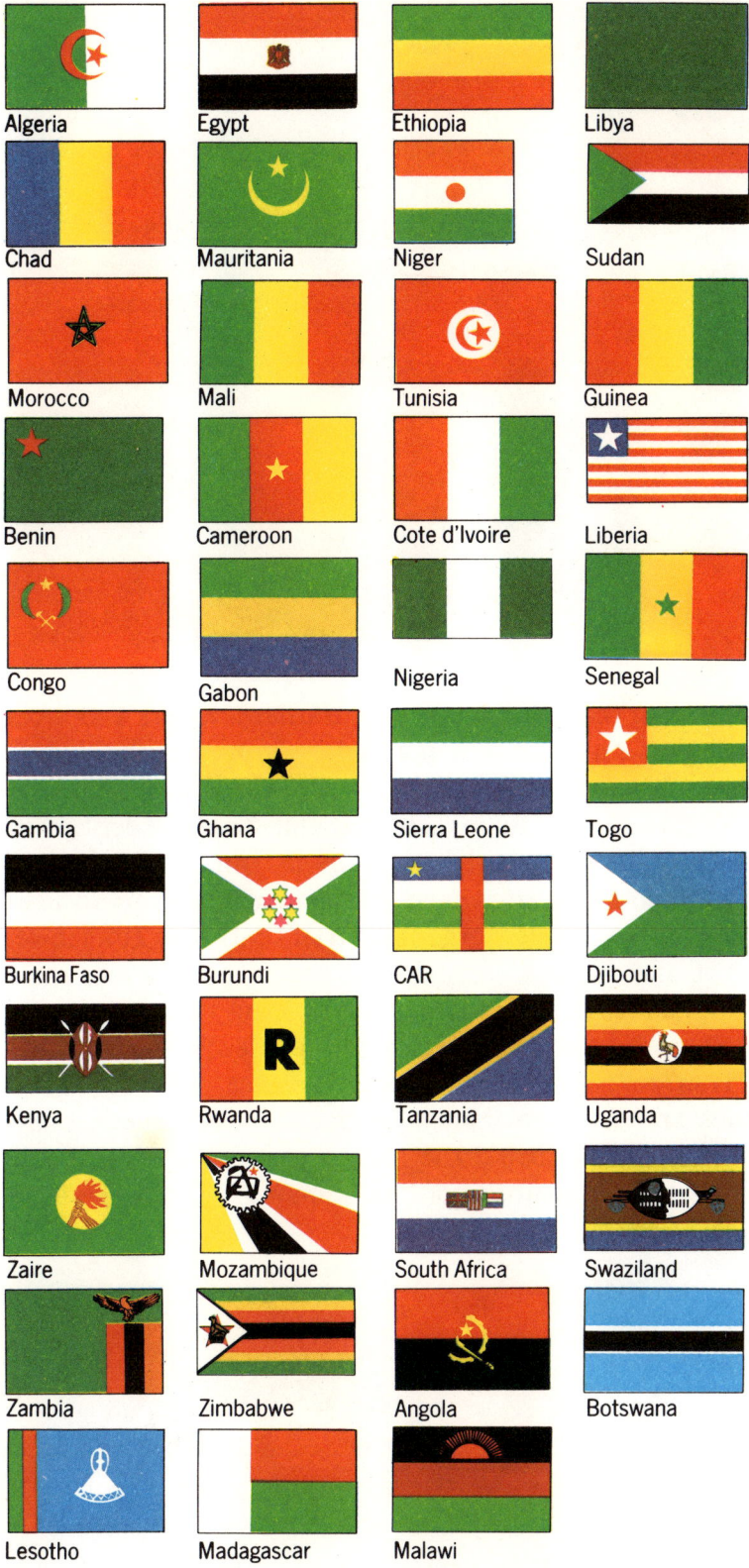

Above: Flags of some African nations. Most of these countries became self-governing in the 1950s and 1960s after being ruled as colonies by Europeans.

33

Above: Africans must grow more food to feed a fast-growing population. Most African farmers, however, still use traditional methods, such as this donkey and camel plough. Few farmers use sophisticated machinery. Where modern methods are used, in parts of South Africa, Zimbabwe and Kenya, they help to increase much needed crop yields.

oil, copper, cobalt, bauxite and uranium. Rivers and lakes are being dammed to make hydro-electricity, and industries are being developed.

Most of Africa's manufacturing industries are centred in South Africa. Industries such as metal producing, machine making and transport manufacturing are located there. There are also large industrial centres in Zimbabwe, Egypt and Algeria. Throughout the rest of Africa, most manufacturing is limited to assembling or making products such as shoes, bicycles and textiles.

Transport systems in much of Africa are poor. Most roads are no more than mud tracks, which become impossible to use during the rainy seasons. Very few people own cars. The majority of rail, shipping and road systems

Ostrich

Zebra

Wildebeest

Left: The Kariba Dam, which lies on the Zambezi River, supplies hydroelectric power to both the industrial centres of Zimbabwe and the copper towns of Zambia. The dam was completed in 1959. The resulting lake flooded an area of about 5200 sq km (2000 sq miles) behind it.

are concentrated in South Africa where they serve the major industrial and business centres.

Fossil remains of the earliest human beings have been found in Africa. In the Nile valley the Ancient Egyptians built one of the greatest early civilizations. But for hundreds of years people in Europe called Africa the 'Dark Continent', because it was so mysterious.

In the 1800s European governments divided Africa into colonies. New ideas and ways of life came to Africa. In time, Africans sought self-government and by the 1960s most colonies had become independent countries.

Many African countries are poor. There are not enough schools and hospitals, and there is not enough food to feed the fast-growing population. There are 12 million new Africans every year. Another problem is the continuation of white-dominated government in South Africa, with its racist *apartheid* laws, though these are being eased.

Africa's rich wildlife astonished the first European explorers. Today lions (*above*) and other game such as zebras, ostriches, wildebeest, buffalo, kudu and crocodiles (*below*) are found in greatly reduced numbers. Game parks are the best hope for their survival.

Buffalo

Kudu

Spur-winged plover

Nile crocodile

 USA

 Canada

 Mexico

 Cuba

 Guatemala

 Nicaragua

 Honduras

 Jamaica

 Costa Rica

 El Salvador

Haiti

 Grenada

 Belize

 Panama

Bahamas

 Barbados

Dominican Republic

Trinidad + Tobago

COUNTRIES

The Americas

North America

North America is the third largest of the Earth's continents. It stretches from the cold wastes of Alaska in the north to the hot deserts of Mexico and the tropical forests of Central America in the south. Canada and the United States of America cover most of North America.

A narrow isthmus, or neck of land, in Central America joins North America to South America. Down the western side of North America run the rugged Rocky Mountains, and there are lower mountain chains in the east. In the centre of the continent are wide grasslands called prairies which occupy vast expanses of land.

The longest river in North America is the Mississippi, which is joined by another long river, the Missouri. The Great Lakes are the largest fresh water lakes in the world. The thundering Niagara Falls plunge 50 metres (164 feet) between two of the Great Lakes.

North America has a wide range of climates. In most of the Arctic lands of the north it is too cold for trees to grow. Farther south are huge forests, first of conifers and then of broad-leaved trees. The central plains have less rainfall, so instead of forests, there are grasslands. In the southwest there are hot deserts, and in the hot, moist isthmus of Panama there are tropical forests.

North America is a continent of great contrasts. It has some of the world's largest cities, but there are also huge areas with hardly any people at all. The United States is the most powerful country in North America.

Above: Flags of the Americas. The two largest nations of North America are the USA and Canada (top).

Right: New York City, with its skyscraping skyline, is the leading business and financial city of North America. Although not the capital of the USA (that is Washington DC), New Yorkers think their city is number one – the 'Big Apple'.

Nome

Alaska

Fairbanks

Anchorage

Greenland

Baffin Is

Whitehorse

Great Bear L.

Juneau

Great Slave L.

Churchill   *Hudson Bay*

CANADA

Rocky

Edmonton

Vancouver

Calgary

L. Winnipeg

Seattle

Regina

PACIFIC OCEAN

Mountains

Winnipeg

Quebec

St. Lawrence

Halifax

Portland

Missouri

Montreal

Ottawa

Toronto

Boston

L. Superior

Minneapolis   St Paul

L. Michigan

L. Huron

L. Erie

L. Ontario

San Francisco

Salt Lake City

Milwaukee

Detroit

Cleveland

New York

Colorado

USA

Chicago

Pittsburg

Philadelphia

Las Vegas

Denver

Indianapolis

Columbus

Baltimore

Washington DC

Los Angeles

Santa Fe

Kansas City

St Louis

BERMUDA

San Diego

Phoenix

Albuquerque

Red

Memphis

Mississippi

Tucson

El Paso

Atlanta

Dallas

Jacksonville

ATLANTIC OCEAN

Sierra Madre

Rio Grande

San Antonio

Houston

New Orleans

G. of California

Miami

Nassau

Gulf of Mexico

BAHAMAS

Monterrey

Havana

CUBA

DOMINICAN

San Juan

MEXICO

HAITI

REP

PUERTO

Port-au-Prince

Santo

RICO

BARBADOS

NORTH AND CENTRAL AMERICA

Guadalajara

JAMAICA

Kingston

Domingo

Mexico City

Caribbean Sea

TRINIDAD & TOBAGO

BELIZE

Belmopan

Port-of-Spain

GUATEMALA

HONDURAS

Guatemala City

Tegucigalpa

NICARAGUA

San Salvador

EL SALVADOR

Managua

Panama Canal Zone

■ Capital Cities

San Jose

Panama

COSTA RICA

PANAMA

0	500	1000 miles

0	500	1000	1500 kilometres

37

Right: Various sources are used to generate the vast amounts of power consumed in the United States each year. This industrial complex is an oil refinery. It is located at Kenai in Central Alaska where there are major oil deposits. Oil is a major source of fuel for domestic heating and industrial power.

Sitting Bull

Geronimo

Above: Two of the American Indian leaders who fought for their tribal lands.

Below: A wagon train of pioneers. During the 1800s thousands of settlers travelled westwards to make their homes in the new lands.

The United States is the most industrialized nation in the world; it makes a quarter of the world's steel, for example. It has rich deposits of minerals including copper, natural gas, uranium, iron ore and coal. Farmland covers nearly half the country and US farmers produce enough grain and other crops to export large quantities to other countries. The capital of the United States is Washington DC, but New York is the largest city. Other important cities are Chicago and Los Angeles.

The United States' northern neighbour is Canada, which is slightly larger but has only about a tenth as many people. Canadians include people of British and French ancestry, and both English and French are official languages. Canada is rich in minerals and has large oil deposits. Its farmers grow cereals and fruit, and rear cattle. Timber comes from Canada's huge forests.

Central America and the West Indies

The people living in Central America and the islands of the West Indies are descendants either of the American Indians or of Europeans and Africans. Most of them speak Spanish, English, French or American Indian languages. In 1492, when Christopher Columbus reached the islands in the Caribbean Sea, he thought he had reached the Indies (Asia), so the islands were named the West Indies.

Central America and the thousands of West Indian islands are mostly hot and mountainous. The climate is ideal for growing fruit, coffee, cotton, tobacco and sugar-cane. Central America's main source of income is from its large plantations, forests and mines. About 10 percent of the world's bananas are produced in the lowland planta-tions. Cuba is the largest of the West Indian islands and it is the third largest producer of sugar in the world.

The countries of Central America include Guatemala, El Salvador, Nicaragua, Panama and Mexico. Mexico was once the home of the Aztecs, and from 1521 to 1822 was ruled by the Spaniards.

The plant and animal life of Central America is similar to that of South America. The lowland rainforests, moun-tains, and the pine and oak forests provide homes for a wide variety of different animal species including the opossum, jaguar, puma, sloth and deer.

Mineral deposits are rich in Central America. Gold and silver, lead and zinc, copper and nickel are found in Nic-aragua and Honduras. There are deposits of natural gas offshore in the Pacific Ocean.

Above: People enjoying a colourful West Indian carnival. This traditional form of outdoor entertainment features music, dance, bright costumes and floats. Carnivals developed from traditional, usually religious, festivals.

The West Indies are divided into two groups of islands. Tobago, along with the Windward and Leeward islands and Trinidad, is part of the Lesser Antilles. The large islands of Cuba, Jamaica, Hispaniola and Puerto Rico make up the Greater Antilles. All the islands are located in an archipelago which lies between North and South America. The climate is tropical, and the vegetation is rich and varied. Much of the land is covered in forest but sugar cane, meat and exotic fruit and vegetables are the main products processed in the manufacturing industries.

SOUTH AMERICA

Barranquilla
Caracas
Maracaibo
Orinoco
Medellin
VENEZUELA
Georgetown
Paramaribo
ATLANTIC OCEAN
Llanos
Cayenne
Bogotá
GUYANA
SURINAM
FRENCH
GUIANA
Cali
COLOMBIA
Quito
ECUADOR
Manáus
Belém
GALAPAGOS IS.
Amazon
Fortaleza
Guayaquil
PERU
Selvas
Recife
Chiclayo
Trujillo
BRAZIL
Salvador
Callão
Lima
Cuzco
BOLIVIA
La Paz
Brazilian Highlands
Cochabamba
Brasilia
Oruro
ANDES
Sucre
PACIFIC OCEAN
Paraná
PARAGUAY
MOUNTAINS
Rio de Janeiro
Gran Chaco
São Paulo
Asunción

Pôrto Alegre
ATLANTIC OCEAN
Córdoba
Mt Aconcagua
URUGUAY
Valparaiso
Rosario
Santiago
Buenos Aires
Montevideo
ARGENTINA
La Plata
CHILE
PAMPAS
Colorado
Bahia Blanca

Chubut

Patagonia

FALKLAND IS.

**Tierra
del Fuego**
Cape Horn

Venezuéla

Colombia

Ecuador

Peru

Bolivia

Chile

Guyana

French Guiana

Paraguay

Brazil

Uruguay

Argentina

■ Capital Cities

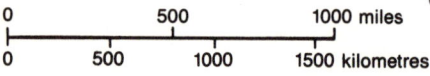

0   500   1000 miles

0   500   1000   1500 kilometres

40

South America

The continent of South America is the fourth largest in the world. There are 13 countries in South America. The largest, Brazil, covers nearly half the continent. The people are descended from the original Indians, or from Europeans and Africans. Most speak Portuguese or Spanish.

The Andes Mountains, the highest in South America, stretch for over 7000 kilometres (4350 miles) down the western side, overlooking the Pacific Ocean. In the Andes is Lake Titicaca, the highest large lake in the world. From the mountains several great rivers flow east across the continent to the Atlantic Ocean. The most important river is the mighty Amazon. Other rivers are the Orinoco, the São Francisco and the River Plate system.

In the centre of the continent are vast plains. They include the rain forests of the Amazon basin, the swamps and lakes of the Gran Chaco, and the grassy pampas of Argentina where gauchos (South American cowboys) herd cattle and horses.

Because it has a variety of climates and soils, South America can produce many kinds of crops. In the hot regions coffee, cocoa, sugar and bananas are grown.

South America is rich in minerals, such as copper, tin, iron, platinum, manganese, nitrates, bauxite, diamonds and emeralds. Mining is an important industry, and there are also large oilfields. South America has some of the largest and fastest-growing cities in the world.

Above: Much of what is known about some of the ancient civilizations of America comes from a type of pictographic writing. It consists of a series of small pictures and was used mainly for making business and historical records. The Incas of Peru, however, had no writing, and sent messages by word of mouth, and by fires and smoke signals. Numerical records were kept using coloured and knotted strings.

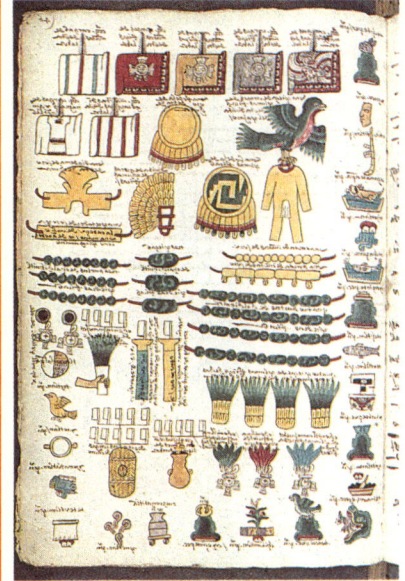

Left: South America has several great cities. Brazil has three of the most important: São Paulo, Rio de Janeiro (shown here) and Brasilia, the national capital. Rio de Janeiro on the Atlantic coast, with its spectacular setting, was the capital of Brazil until 1960 when the new city of Brasília, designed by Lucia Costa and Oscar Niemeyer, was made the capital.

Below: China is the world's third largest country. It has many different landscapes. About 43 per cent of the land area is covered by mountains. Other types of land-forms include tropical rain forests, grasslands and deserts. These diverse habitats support a wide range of plants and animals. Here, lotus plants are growing on the lower land, while mountains rise steeply in the background.

More than one fifth of the world's total population lives in China. The population is mainly Han Chinese and is of Mongoloid stock. China is a mainly rural, agricultural nation, although many of its major cities have gained great importance as industrially productive centres. There are more than 30 cities in China with populations of more than one million people.

Asia

Asia is the largest continent, stretching from the Arctic to the Equator. It covers nearly a third of the Earth's land surface. With a population of over 2500 million, Asia has more than half of the world's people.

There are many different types of land and climate in Asia. In the north are evergreen forests, flat grasslands called steppes and cold tundra plains. Most of this area is called Siberia and is part of the former Soviet Union. In central Asia are the world's highest mountains, including the mighty Himalaya Mountains. The high plains of Tibet are known as 'the roof of the world'. From these mountains many great rivers flow into the rest of Asia. Asia has some of the world's longest rivers. They include the Ob, Lena and Yenisey in the north; the Euphrates in the west; the Indus, Ganges, Brahmaputra, Salween, Irrawaddy and Mekong in the south; and the Huang He and Chang Jiang (Yangtze) in the east.

Some parts of Asia are very dry. There are wide deserts, such as the cold Gobi Desert of Mongolia and the hot deserts of India and Arabia. There the land is dry and barren. In other places there is heavy rainfall, but only once a year during the monsoon season. The rain is brought by the monsoon winds blowing onto the land from the sea.

Left: The city palace is one of the most spectacular buildings in Jaipur, India. Jaipur is often called the 'pink city' because of the colour of many of its buildings, and is one of the most beautiful cities in India. Founded in November 1727 by Maharaja Sawai Jai Singh II, Jaipur became the capital city of the state of Rajasthan in northern India in 1949. It is a busy and prosperous commercial centre and is famous for stone, marble and ivory carving, brass, textiles, jewellery and fine enamel work.

Few people live in the mountains, plains and deserts. Those who do are mostly nomads (wanderers), grazing flocks of sheep, goats, horses and camels. Almost all Asia's people live either in the fertile river valleys, or on the coastal plains. Most of them are peasant farmers, scraping a living out of a small patch of land. But more and more people are going to live in the cities.

In the warm, wet monsoon lands of southern Asia, rice is the chief crop. Rice and fish are the main foods of many Asians. Other crops are tea, sugar, cotton, coffee and spices. In countries like Bangladesh many of the people are very poor. There are too many people for the land to support, so they cannot grow enough food. If the crops fail because of flood or drought, many people may starve.

Asia has few large industries, but valuable raw materials. The forests provide timber and rubber. There are minerals such as coal, iron, copper and tin. In southwest Asia some countries (such as Saudi Arabia and Kuwait) have become rich because there is oil beneath the desert. The countries of the Middle East, where Europe and Asia meet, include Israel, Lebanon, Syria and Turkey.

The most important industrial country of Asia is Japan, which manufactures many products to sell in other countries. China and India are gradually developing their industries, as well as improving their agriculture.

China has a history going back 3500 years and it has more people than any other country. It was once an

Below: A Japanese temple. Buddhism and Shinto are the main religions in Japan. In the late 1900s Shinto was made a state religion. It emphasized the worship of the emperor as a divinity. All Japanese, regardless of their religion were, at that time, forced to worship at Shinto shrines. The country has many shrines and temples. The Japanese often make pilgrimages to these places of worship with offerings of fruit and flowers.

ASIA

Area: 44,418,500 sq km
Population: 3,000,000,000
Highest mountain: Everest 8848 m

Principal lakes: Caspian Sea, Aral Sea, Baikal

Principal rivers: Yangtze, Tigris, Euphrates, Indus, Ganges

Countries: 41 and part of the former Soviet Union, part of Turkey, part of Egypt

ARCTIC OCEAN

Yenisey

Lena

RUSSIA AND THE
FORMER REPUBLICS OF THE USSR

URAL MOUNTAINS

Ob

Omsk

Novosibirsk

L. Baikal

Irkutsk

BLACK
SEA

Ankara

Izmir

TURKEY

CYPRUS

Nicosia

Beirut

LEBANON

Jerusalem

ISRAEL

Amman

JORDAN

Aleppo

SYRIA

Damascus

CAUCASUS

CASPIAN
SEA

Aral Sea

Syr Darya

L. Balkhash

Ulan Bator

MONGOLIA

TIEN SHAN

GOBI DESERT

CHINA

He

Huang

Lanzhou

Xi'an

Tigris

Euphrates

Baghdad

IRAQ

Basra

Abadan

Kuwait

KUWAIT

Tehran

Isfahan

IRAN

Amu Darya

AFGHANISTAN

Kabul

Islamabad

Lahore

KASHMIR

TIBET

Chengdu

Chongqui

RED SEA

Medina

Jidda

Mecca

Riyadh

ARABIAN
DESERT

SAUDI ARABIA

BAHRAIN

QATAR

Doha

U.A.E.

OMAN

Muscat

PAKISTAN

Indus

Karachi

Hyderabad

Ahmadabad

Delhi

New Delhi

Kanpur

Lucknow

Varanasi

Ganges

HIMALAYAS

NEPAL

Katmandu

Mt.
Everest

Lhasa

Thimphu

BHUTAN

Salween

Brahmaputra

Dacca

Calcutta

Irrawaddy

Mandalay

Hanoi

LAOS

Xi Jian

Kunming

Chang Jiang (Yangtze)

Saná

YEMEN

Aden

INDIA

Godavari

Nagpur

BANGLA
-DESH

MYANMAR
(Burma)

Yangon

Chiang Mai

THAILAND

Vientiane

VIET

Mekong

CAMBOD

Phnom Penh

Saic

ARABIAN SEA

Bombay

Hyderabad

Bangalore

Madras

BAY OF
BENGAL

Bangkok

GULF OF
THAILA

SRI LANKA

Colombo

MALDIVE IS.

Malé

■ Capital Cities

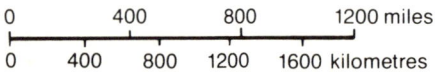

0   400   800   1200 miles
0   400 800 1200 1600 kilometres

INDIAN OCEAN

Penang

Medan

Padang

MALAY

Kuala Lum

SINGAPOR

Sumatra

Jakarta

J

44

SEA OF OKHOTSK

Amur

Hokkaido
Sapporo

Harbin

Vladivostok

SEA OF JAPAN

JAPAN

Beijing
Dalian

NORTH KOREA
Pyongyang

Honshu

Tokyo
Yokohama
Kyoto
Osaka
Kobe

SOUTH KOREA
Seoul
Pusan

Tientsin

Kitakyushu

Nagasaki

Kyushu

Nanjing

Shanghai

EAST CHINA SEA

Wuhan

PACIFIC OCEAN

Taipei
TAIWAN

Guangzhou

HONG KONG
MACAO

Luzon

SOUTH CHINA SEA

Manila
Quezon City

PHILIPPINES

Mindanao

BRUNEI
Bandar Seri Begawan

Sarawak

West Irian

Sulawesi

Borneo

INDONESIA

Surabaya
Timor

Iran

China

India

Brunei

Iraq

Mongolia

Nepal

Laos

Israel

South Korea

Sri Lanka

Thailand

Jordan

North Korea

Bangladesh

Indonesia

Kuwait

Afghanistan

Myanmar (Burma)

Pakistan

Lebanon

Bhutan

Vietnam

Singapore

UAE

Oman

Saudi Arabia

Malaysia

Philippines

Yemen

Syria

Bahrain

Japan

Maldives

Turkey

Cyprus

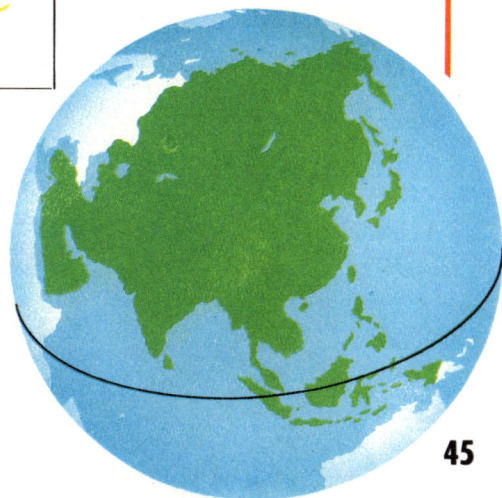

45

Above: An Indian farmer ploughing. Farming, particularly wheat and rice-growing, is important in India. About seven out of ten of its people earn their living by farming. Most farms are small, and the farmers still use traditional methods. There are also millions of cattle and water buffalo; these animals are sacred to the Hindus.

empire, but is now a republic. Japan too has a long history. Though it lacks natural resources such as coal and oil, it is one of the world's wealthiest industrial nations. Ten Japanese cities have populations of over a million. India, Bangladesh and Pakistan are three of the most densely populated countries in the world. India has the second largest population, after China, and (like China) India has an ancient history. It is the world's largest democracy.

The great religions of Christianity, Islam, Hinduism and Buddhism all began in Asia. The Asian peoples reached high levels of progress in the arts and sciences long before Europeans did so. But the deserts and mountains kept the

Below: In southeast Asia rice is grown in flooded paddy fields. Hillsides are planted in terraces with mudbrick banks.

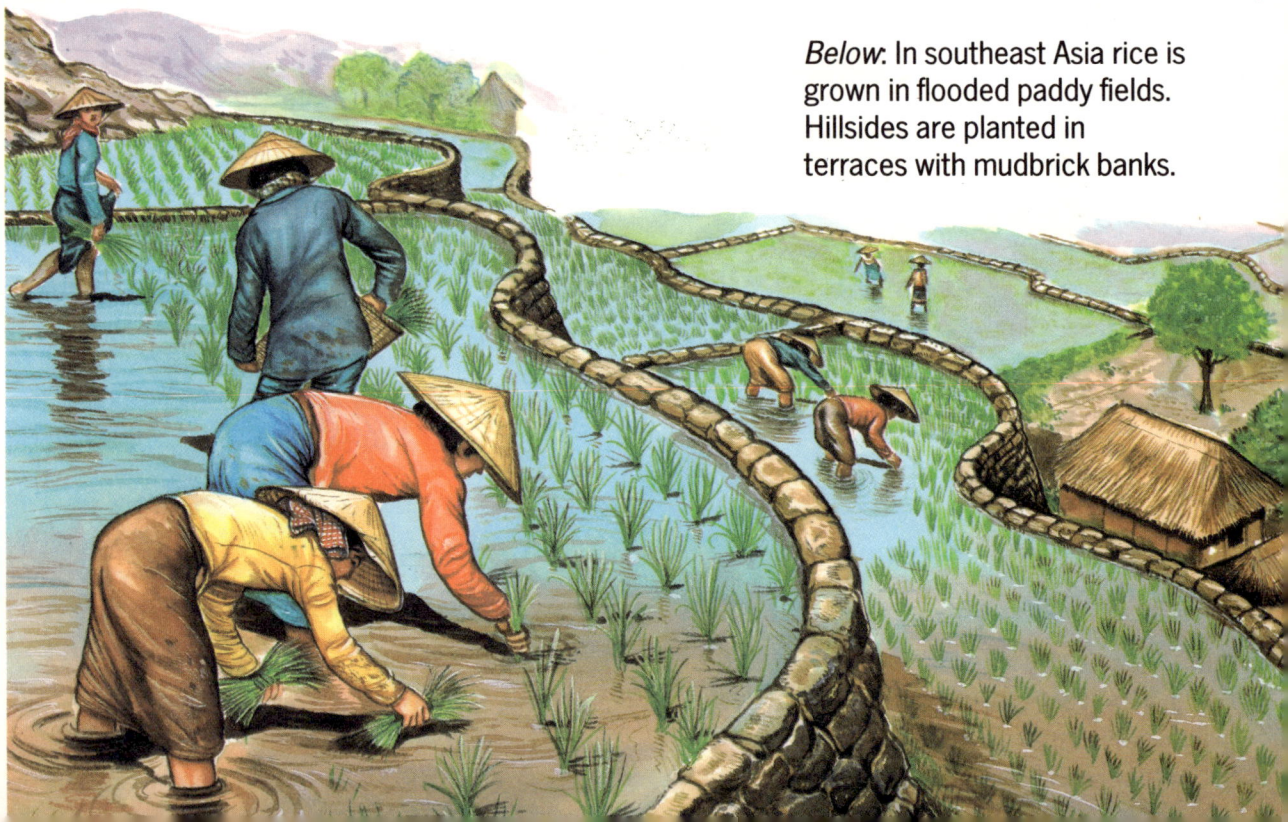

Left: Hong Kong is a prosperous commercial centre located on the southeast coast of China. It is currently a British dependency but will be returned to China in 1997.

Indian elephant

peoples of Asia apart, for only camel caravans could cross the dangerous lands between them. So each part of Asia developed its own languages, customs and ways of life.

European explorers came to Asia in search of riches and spices. They set up trading stations, and later founded colonies. Some parts of Asia were ruled by Europeans until modern times. But now all the countries of Asia are independent. The people of southeast Asia, notably in Vietnam and Cambodia, have suffered from wars in modern times. There have been political problems in Burma, Indonesia and the Philippines, and hostility between communist North Korea and non-communist South Korea.

Indian cobra

Below: Indonesian schoolgirls attend lessons given outside at a typical elementary school in Bali.

Right: Some Asian wild animals. Many of their habitats are threatened by human activities.

Tiger

Giant panda

ANIMALS OF ASIA

Australasia

The greater part of Australasia is Australia, much of which is empty desert. The next two countries in order of size are Papua New Guinea and New Zealand. Both have more people per square kilometre than Australia, though neither is densely populated. There are also about 30,000 Pacific Ocean islands. Some, like Fiji and Western Samoa, are fairly densely populated. Others are uninhabited.

The islands in the Pacific Ocean are grouped according to their original inhabitants. These groups are Melanesia, Micronesia and Polynesia. Melanesia means 'black islands' and the people on these islands have dark skin and frizzy hair. This group includes Papua New Guinea, the Solomon Islands and Fiji. Micronesia means 'little islands'. The Micronesian islands are north of Melanesia, and include Nauru and Wake, the Caroline, Kiribati, Mariana and Marshall islands. The people have straight hair and copper-coloured skin. Polynesia, which means 'many islands', spreads over a wide area. It is bounded by New Zealand in the southwest, Easter Island in the southeast and Hawaii in the north. The Polynesians are taller than the other Pacific Islanders and have light brown skin. They include the Maoris of New Zealand.

Two large islands, the North and South Islands, and several smaller islands make up New Zealand. Probably the Maoris settled there about 1000 years ago. Later Europeans came. About 70 per cent of New Zealanders live in the North Island, many of them on the fertile plains by the coast. Wellington, the capital, is on North Island, as is the largest city, Auckland.

Above: An Australian Aborigine. These people probably came from Asia and drove out the native inhabitants of Australia. In the late 1700s, when the first Europeans settled in Australia, there were about 300,000 Aborigines. There were more than 500 tribes, each with its own language. Today there are fewer than 100,000, which is less than one percent of the country's population. Few Aborigines continue to follow traditional ways but some have returned to traditional homelands in northern and central Australia.

Right: Captain Cook and his men were met by the warlike Maoris when they explored New Zealand in 1769. Although Cook took possession of the islands, colonization did not begin for several decades.

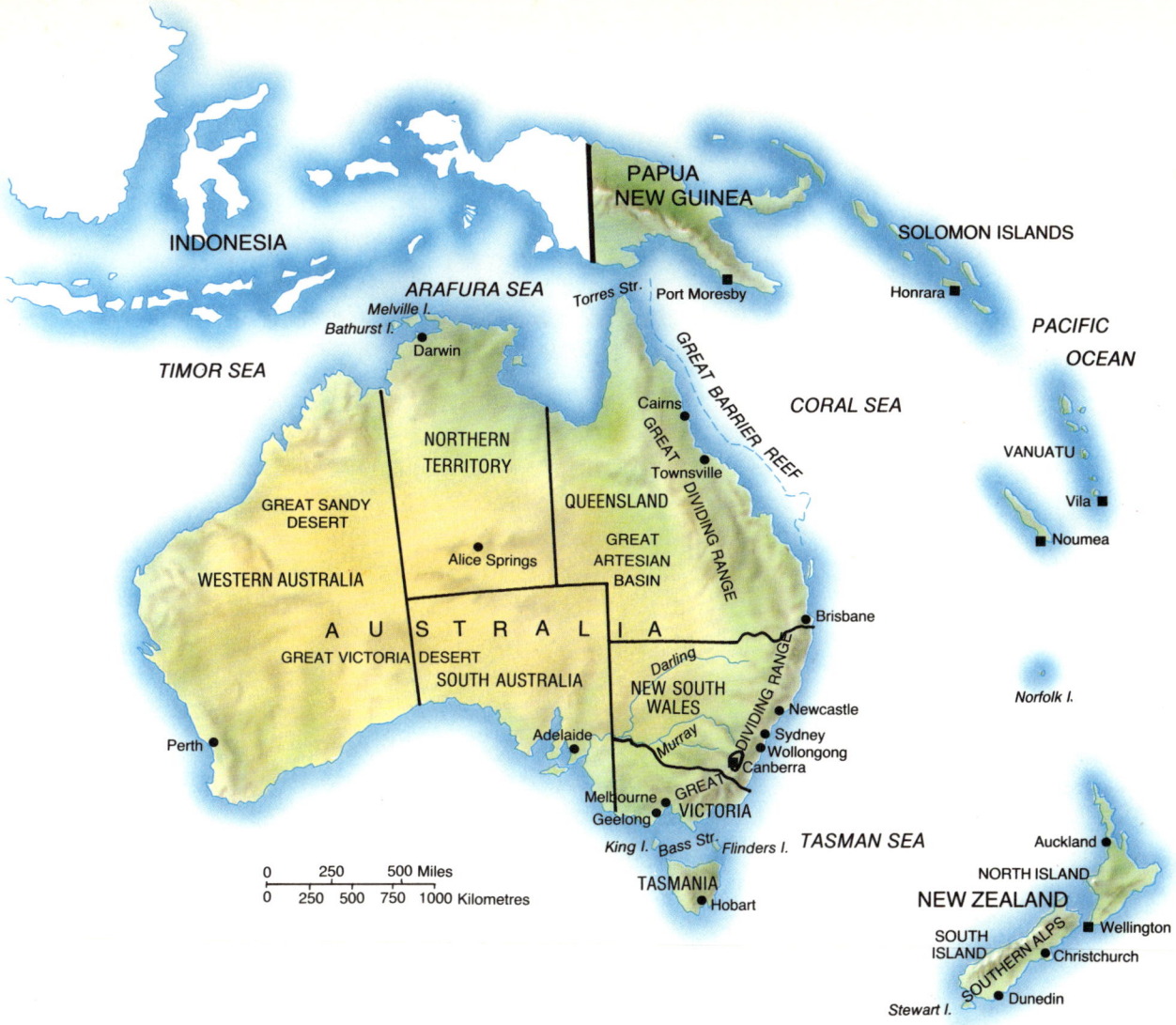

PAPUA
NEW GUINEA

INDONESIA

SOLOMON ISLANDS

ARAFURA SEA

Torres Str.   Port Moresby

Honrara

PACIFIC

OCEAN

Melville I.

Bathurst I.

Darwin

TIMOR SEA

Cairns

CORAL SEA

GREAT BARRIER REEF

NORTHERN
TERRITORY

GREAT DIVIDING RANGE

Townsville

VANUATU

Vila

Noumea

GREAT SANDY
DESERT

QUEENSLAND

GREAT
ARTESIAN
BASIN

WESTERN AUSTRALIA

A U S T R A L I A

GREAT VICTORIA DESERT

Brisbane

SOUTH AUSTRALIA

Darling

Norfolk I.

NEW SOUTH
WALES

Newcastle

GREAT DIVIDING RANGE

Alice Springs

Perth

Adelaide

Murray

Sydney
Wollongong
Canberra

Melbourne

GREAT

Geelong   VICTORIA

King I. Bass Str. Flinders I.

TASMAN SEA

Auckland

NORTH ISLAND

NEW ZEALAND

0   250   500 Miles
0 250 500 750 1000 Kilometres

TASMANIA

Hobart

SOUTH
ISLAND

SOUTHERN ALPS

Wellington

Christchurch

Stewart I.   Dunedin

Below: The harsh, yet beautiful landscape of the Australian wilderness, or outback. The red rock outcrops are typical features of the Australian desert. The sparse vegetation consists mainly of coarse grass and dry bushes.

49

Australia

New Zealand

Nauru

Solomon Islands

Tuvalu

Western Samoa

Fiji

Kiribati

Papua-New Guinea

Tonga

Vanuatu

Above: Maori woodcarvings. Maoris were New Zealand's first people. Today, there are about 290,000 Maoris living in New Zealand making up the largest minority group.

Right: Mount Cook, in South Island, is the highest peak in New Zealand. It rises from the main range of mountains, the Southern Alps, to a height of 3764 metres (12,349 feet). The mountain is rugged, and glaciers lie in its upper valleys, high above the thick forests.

The climate is mild. Two-thirds of the people live in towns, but farming is the main activity. Leading exports are wool, beef, lamb, mutton and dairy products. Most of New Zealand's electricity comes from hydro-electric power stations situated in both the North and South Islands.

Australia is a very flat empty country. To the west there are plateaus, most of which are desert. There are vast, dry plains in the centre, and highlands in the east and southeast. The famous Great Barrier Reef, the largest coral reef in the world, runs along the northeastern coast. More than half the people live in the four largest cities (Sydney, Melbourne, Brisbane and Adelaide).

The first people in Australia were probably the Tasmanian Aborigines. They were driven south to the island of Tasmania by the Australian Aborigines who probably originated in Asia. In 1788 Britain set up a convict settlement in Sydney. The first free settlers arrived in 1793, and the numbers of British immigrants soon increased. After the Second World War (1939–45), settlers began to arrive from other European countries, such as Greece and Yugo-

Kookaburra

Above: The Fijian people make good use of the palm trees for traditional crafts and buildings.

Right: Some of Australasia's native animals. The kiwi is the only known bird that has nostrils at the end of its bill.

Tasmanian devil

Koala

Kiwi

Above: Bora Bora is one of the Pacific Islands. It belongs to France. The island was made by volcanoes.

Kangaroo

slavia. There are also people of Asian origin who have settled in Australia.

Australia is a leading producer of bauxite, iron ore and lead, while other metals, coal and oil are also mined. Australia's 150 million sheep produce wool which, along with wheat, beef and dairy products, is one of Australia's chief agricultural exports. The many climates in Australia (from the tropical north to temperate Tasmania) enable a variety of crops, including sugarcane, barley, rice and potatoes, to be grown. Industry is also becoming important, chiefly in the south and east.

AUSTRALASIAN ANIMALS 51

Above: During the late 1980s almost one million East Germans, dissatisfied with their lives under communist control, fled through the open borders of Czechoslovakia and Austria to political freedom in the West. As a result of this exodus, the East German government was forced to promise reforms and in November 1989 it relaxed travel restrictions and opened East Germany's borders. Almost immediately the people of East and West Berlin began to pull down the Berlin Wall, which had for almost 29 years divided the city into two. Germany was reunited in October 1990.

Europe

In order of size among the world's continents, Europe comes sixth. However, in order of population, Europe comes second. One-sixth of the world's people lives in Europe. Only Asia, which is four times the size of Europe, has a higher population.

Most of Europe has a mild and pleasant climate, neither very cold in winter nor too hot in summer. There are some inhospitable regions. The Arctic regions of northern Europe are very cold, but the northwestern shores are warmed by the waters of the North Atlantic Drift. The countries by the Mediterranean Sea in the south are very warm. Europe has a wide variety of plant life, with many different kinds of flowers, shrubs and trees. The scenery often changes rapidly as the traveller moves from mountains to valleys, from flat plains to neatly ploughed fields. There are wide fertile grasslands, especially in the east, and some thick forests of conifers and broad-leaved trees, although much of the ancient forest has been cleared to make way for cities, factories and farms.

Europe has high mountains, such as the Alps and Pyrenees in the west, and the Urals and Caucasus in the east which divide Europe from Asia. The highest mountain is Mount Elbruz in the Caucasus Mountains. It is 5633 metres (18,480 feet) high. Europe's biggest lake is the Caspian Sea. Both of the above are in the former Soviet Union. Much of northern Europe consists of lowlands or

EUROPE

ARCTIC OCEAN

Murmansk

Narvik

ICELAND

Reykjavik

NORWEGIAN SEA

Arkhangelsk

FAROE IS.

KJOLEN MOUNTAINS

SWEDEN   FINLAND

Trondheim

L. Onega

SHETLAND IS.

Tampere

NORWAY   Sundsvall

Vyborg

L. Ladoga

Helsinki

ORKNEY IS.

Bergen

Leningrad

Aberdeen

Oslo   Stockholm

ESTONIA

Novgorod

Yaroslavl

NORTH SEA

Stavanger

Vänern

Glasgow   Edinburgh

Vättern

LATVIA

Moscow

Belfast

Gothenburg

BALTIC SEA

Riga

IRELAND   UNITED
           KINGDOM

DENMARK

Dvina

Smolensk

Dublin   Manchester

Copenhagen   Malmö

LITHUANIA

RUSSIA AND THE
FORMER REPUBLICS
OF THE USSR

Cork

Birmingham

Hamburg

Kaliningrad

Minsk

Cardiff London

Gdansk

Kharkov

NETHER
-LANDS

Elbe

Poznan

Vistula

Warsaw

Kiev

Thames

Amster
dam

Berlin

ATLANTIC OCEAN

Rhine

GERMANY

Dnepr

English Channel

Brussels

POLAND

Kraków

Dnepropetrovsk

Le Havre BELGIUM

Bonn

Dnestr

Brest

Paris

Frankfurt

Prague

Dnestr

Odessa

LUX—
EMBOURG

Stuttgart

CZECHOSLOVAKIA

Prut

CARPATHIANS

Nantes

Loire

Seine

Munich

Vienna

Saône

Bern

Zurich

AUSTRIA

Budapest

FRANCE

Geneva

SWITZ-
ERLAND

Milan

LIECHTENSTEIN

HUNGARY

ROMANIA

La Coruña

Bordeaux

Lyons

Rhône

Po

Turin

Zagreb

Bucharest

BLACK SEA

Santander

Toulouse

MONACO

Venice

Trieste

Bilbao

Nice

Belgrade

Danube

BULGARIA

Oporto

Valladolid

PYRENEES

Marseille

Florence

YUGOSLAVIA

Douro

ANDORRA

SAN MARINO

Dubrovnik

Sofia

Lisbon

Madrid

Ebro

Corsica

ITALY

Rome

ALBANIA

Istanbul

Tagus

Barcelona

Ajaccio

TURKEY

Guidiana

Valencia

Naples

Bari

Tirana

Thessaloniki

PORTUGAL

SPAIN

BALEARIC IS.

Sardinia

Taranto

Seville

Cagliari

GREECE

Cadiz

Malaga

Palermo

Messina

GIBRALTAR

Sicily

Athens

MALTA

Crete

MEDITERRANEAN SEA

■ Capital Cities

| 0 | 100 | 200 | 300 | 400 miles |

| 0 | 200 | 400 | 600 Kilometres |

53

Right: Europe is famous for wine-making. The main European wine producing countries are Germany, Spain, Greece, Italy and France. In the wine-making process, ripe grapes are harvested when they contain the maximum amount of sugar (this is tested using special equipment). Bunches of grapes are harvested with a sharp knife and taken to the crusher or wine-press. The resulting mixture of grape skins, pips and juice is then put into the fermenting vats. After fermentation the wine is run into barrels. It is refined several times, stored for a while, and later bottled.

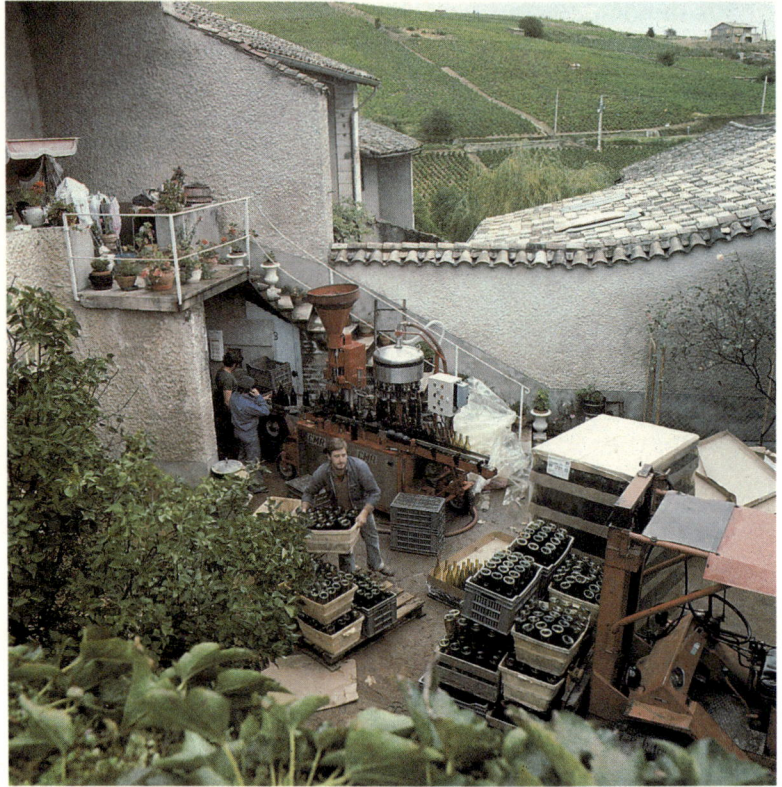

Below: The Leaning Tower of Pisa has been sinking sideways since it was completed in 1350. The lean of the tower has increased about 30 cm during the past 100 years. It is one of Italy's most famous tourist attractions.

rolling hills and river valleys. Some land is very flat and low-lying. About 40 per cent of the Netherlands is below sea level. Much of the continent has rich soil that produces high crop yields. Today, there are few parts of Europe that remain undeveloped.

Eastern Europe has only a few big rivers, but they can be navigated by river craft for long distances. Chief among these eastern rivers are the Volga and Danube. Western European rivers include the Rhine. The west coast of Europe is washed by the Atlantic Ocean. Europe has good rainfall, and there are no deserts. Much of the land is very fertile. Cereals, fruit and vegetables can be grown well, and there is good pasture for cattle and sheep. There are also a number of valuable minerals, such as coal and iron ore.

Throughout its long history, Europe has been settled by many different peoples. The Ancient Greeks and Romans were the two most influential European civilizations. Since that time Europe has been a centre of art and learning. It is often called the birthplace of Western civilization. Europe is a continent of great cities, such as London, Paris, Moscow, Rome, Athens and Vienna. Many European cities are hundreds of years old, and their castles, churches and museums are full of fascinating history. But there are also tiny villages, sometimes even older and full of interest

for the visitor. Millions of tourists journey around Europe each year to look at its historical treasures.

The people of Europe are made up of many different nationalities. The European part of the former Soviet Union (the rest being in Asia) is the biggest country in Europe. The Vatican City is the smallest European country. The people of Europe speak many languages. There are three main language groups: the Romance languages (such as Italian, French and Spanish); the Balto-Slavic languages (such as Russian and Polish); and the Germanic and Scandinavian languages (which include German, Swedish and Danish). But there are other small languages, such as Scottish Gaelic which belongs to the Celtic group. A number of people living in Europe are of African, Caribbean, or Asian origin.

This variety of peoples accounts for the richness of Europe's culture. In the past, differences between nations often led to quarrels and to war. European wars often affected the rest of the world, because some of the countries of Europe were very powerful. The strongest countries, such as Britain and France, built up large empires overseas from the 1600s. Today, Europeans no longer rule overseas empires. Since World War II (1939–45), which left much of Europe in ruins, the countries of Europe have

Prague (*above*), capital of Czechoslovakia, and Moscow (*below*), capital of the former USSR, are rich cultural centres with many museums and beautiful historic buildings.

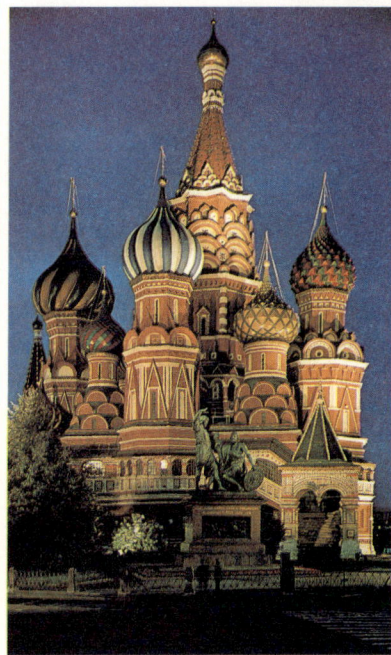

55

Right: Switzerland has now become a popular destination for winter as well as summer holidays. Every year from late December to April, towns and villages in the Alps become full of skiers looking for excitement on the slopes, and traditional food and hospitality in the evenings. In the past few years, however, mild winters have caused a severe lack of snow in the early part of the season. Some resorts have installed machines to create snow artificially.

Above: The historic island of Sardinia attracts many thousands of tourists every year. It is popular for its beautiful beaches and hot summers. An Italian island, Sardinia keeps up many of its ancient customs and traditions. It lies in the Mediterranean Sea about 160 km (100 miles) from the Italian mainland. Sardinia is the second largest of the Mediterranean islands.

56

tried to live in peace. Divisions between the communist countries of the east and the free nations of the west have begun to break down, with the ending of the 'cold war'.

Twelve countries of western Europe belong to an economic and trading association called the European Community, sometimes known as the Common Market. Its aim is to remove trade barriers between members, and to make Europe as powerful in international trade as Japan and the United States.

Europe lives by trade. Although it has some of the most modern and efficient farms in the world, Europe cannot grow enough food to feed its population of more than 700 million people. Ever since the Industrial Revolution of the 1700s and 1800s, which began in Europe, the countries of

Norway

Denmark

Finland

Iceland

Sweden

United Kingdom

Ireland

Luxembourg

Belgium

Austria

France

Italy

Monaco

Andorra

Portugal

Spain

Netherlands

Germany

Switzerland

San Marino

Vatican City

Malta

Greece

Estonia

Albania

Poland

Czechoslovakia

Hungary

Latvia

Lithuania

Russia

Bulgaria

Romania

Yugoslavia

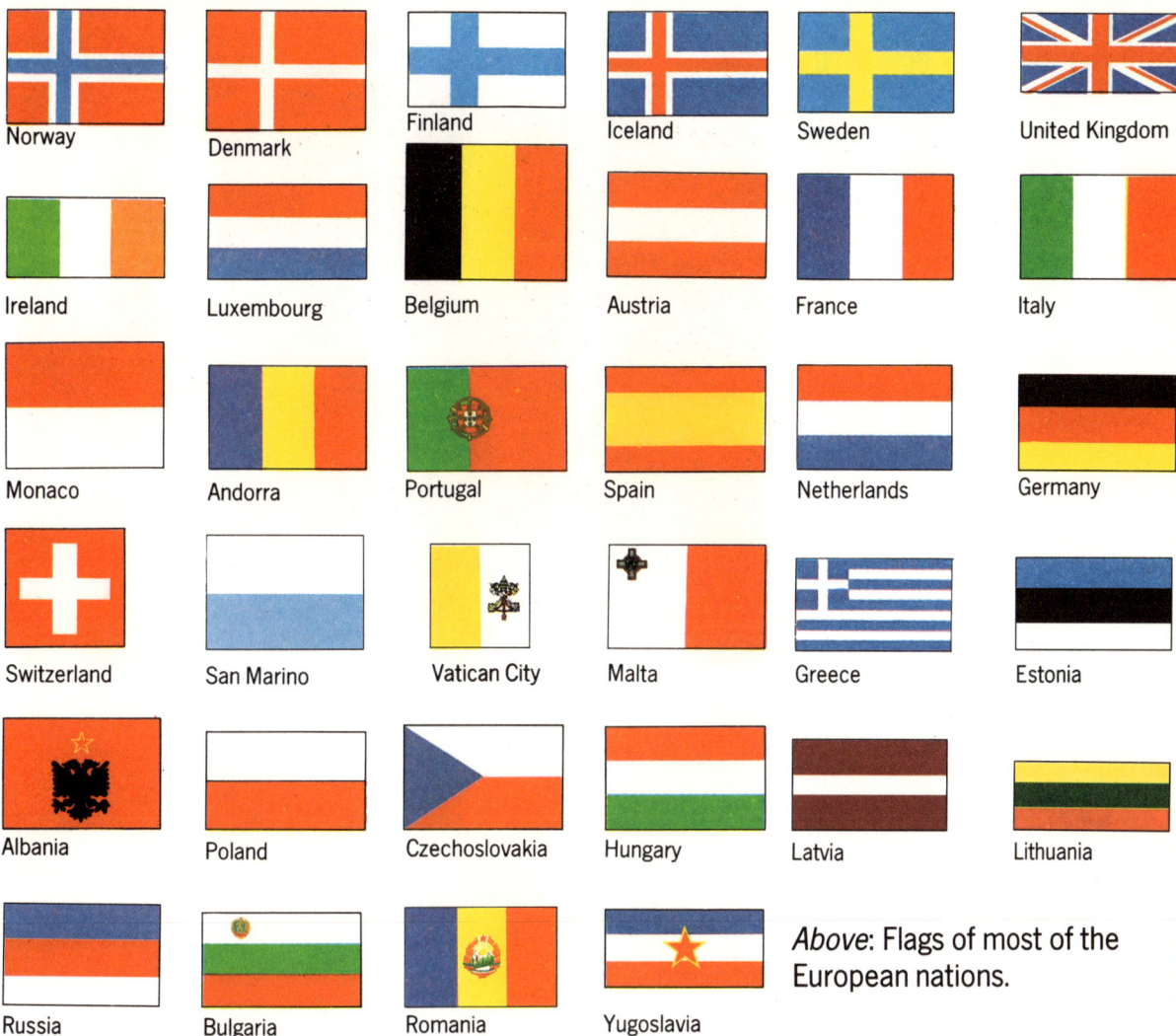

Above: Flags of most of the European nations.

Below: A beautiful and colourful way of preserving old traditions – the Swedish national costume.

Europe have relied more and more on industry. There are many factories, making all kinds of goods. European workers make aircraft, vehicles, machinery, electrical goods, textiles, clothing, processed food and other manufactured goods for sale all over the world. Europe is also a centre for banking and finance. Most of Europe's people live and work in towns and cities.

Europe has good roads, railways, airports and canals. Ships carry goods across the Baltic Sea, the North Sea and the Mediterranean Sea, and Europe has some of the world's busiest ports, such as Rotterdam in the Netherlands. In the 1400s and 1500s the search for new trade links encouraged European merchants to explore Africa, Asia and America. Later, European countries started colonies in these areas, and in the 1800s millions of poor people left Europe to begin new lives as settlers in the

Right: The fishing industry is very important to Europe as it provides jobs and food for millions of people. Limits are fixed to protect species such as haddock and cod from being overfished. Although all the coastal waters are fished, the chief fishing grounds include the North Sea, the Baltic Sea and the polar waters of the Arctic Ocean.

Below: Friesian cows are bred on Europe's farms mainly for dairy foods. They are characterized by their black and white markings. The two colours are defined in two distinct patches. They have horns and a large body, and develop and mature within two years.

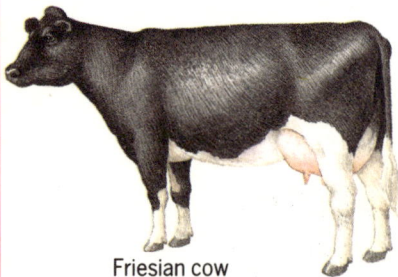

Friesian cow

Right: Much of the Netherlands is low lying and flat. About two thirds of the land is farm land. Dairy farming is a major industry. There are almost five and a half million cattle in the Netherlands, most of them are Friesians.

United States, Canada and Australia. European ideas, languages and discoveries spread throughout the world.

Today, the different nations of Europe are coming closer together. Travel and television have helped break down old national barriers. People visit each other's countries, eat similar foods, and enjoy the same entertainment – such as soccer. National costume is worn nowadays only on special or ceremonial occasions, and the people shopping in a city street in Birmingham (England), Dusseldorf (Germany) or Milan (Italy) look much the same. Yet this small continent, with about 70 people to every square kilometre of land, still reveals amazing variety.

Bicoloured
white-toothed
shrew

Reindeer

Teal

female

male

Otter

Left and above: Animals commonly found in Europe. Much of Europe now has few large animals. Wolves and bears, for instance, are almost extinct. Reindeer are kept in herds by the people of Lapland for their hides and meat.

Because Europe is such a crowded continent, there is little room now for the large wild animals such as bison, bears, deer and wolves that were once common. Their habitats have been destroyed in most areas to provide land for building or cultivation. Smaller mammals and birds are still plentiful, and there are fish in the rivers, lakes and seas. In parts of Europe, homes and factories threaten to engulf the countryside. Pesticides and fertilizers used in intensive farming also harm the ecological system. Pollution of soil, air and water is a serious problem in some areas. Europeans must work hard to protect the environment which they share with animals.

Below: Nocturnal (night-time) animals found in the fields and woodlands of northern Europe. In order to survive through the cold weather of winter, hedgehogs and bats hibernate or go into a deep sleep. Their heartbeats and breathing are slowed down and they live off stored fat until the spring. Foxes grow thicker coats during these months.

Nightjar

Bat

Fox

Badger

Rabbit

Weasel

Hedgehog

59

Right: Within the Arctic Circle is the 'land of the midnight Sun'. In midsummer, the Sun never sets. It sinks close to the horizon at midnight, but never actually sets. So there is daylight for 24 hours. In midwinter, the Sun never rises and there is day-long darkness.

Below: Polar bears live in the Arctic. Their white fur camouflages them against the snow, and they have hair on the soles of their feet to help them grip on slippery ice.

8 pm 9 pm 10 pm 11 pm Midnight 1 am 2 am 3 am 4 am

Polar bear

Below: The wilderness of Antarctica is surprisingly rich in animal life. Birds and seals feed on fish which are plentiful in the cold plankton-rich ocean.

Polar Regions

The Earth has two polar regions, both cold and mostly snow-covered. The area around the North Pole is called the Arctic. Most of it consists of the Arctic Ocean, which is frozen for much of the year. Winters are long and bitterly cold, and for months the Sun never rises. However, in the short, mild summer, the Sun never sets and the warm south winds blow. As the ice melts, brightly coloured flowers, moss, and small bushes grow. Eskimo and Lapp people live in the Arctic.

The Antarctic is a vast ice-covered continent, one and a half times as big as the United States of America. It is the coldest continent in the world. Plant life grows only near the coast where ice and snow melt in summer. But the seas are rich in life, including fish, whales, seals and penguins. There are many sea birds in the Antarctic, some of which fly north to warmer lands when winter comes. The only people who live there work at weather stations and research bases. However, tourists now fly in to visit Antarctica, and in future minerals may be mined there.

Adelie penguins

Emperor penguin

Albatross

Crabeater seal

Arctic Map (North Polar Region)

ACIFIC OCEAN

ALASKA (USA)

BERING STRAIT

WRANGEL ISLAND

EAST SIBERIAN SEA

CANADA

BEAUFORT SEA

NEW SIBERIAN ISLANDS

LAPTEV SEA

BANKS ISLAND

ARCTIC OCEAN

USSR

VICTORIA

QUEEN ELIZABETH ISLANDS

NORTH POLE

SEVERNAYA ZEMLYA

ELLESMERE ISLAND

BAFFIN ISLAND

Thule

FRANZ JOSEF LAND

BAFFIN BAY

NOVAYA ZEMLYA

GREENLAND (DENMARK)

SVALBARD (NORWAY)

GREENLAND SEA

BARENTS SEA

Godthaab

Hammerfest

Murmansk

ARCTIC CIRCLE

Tromso

LAPLAND

ANTIC OCEAN

Reykjavik ICELAND

NORWAY SWEDEN FINLAND

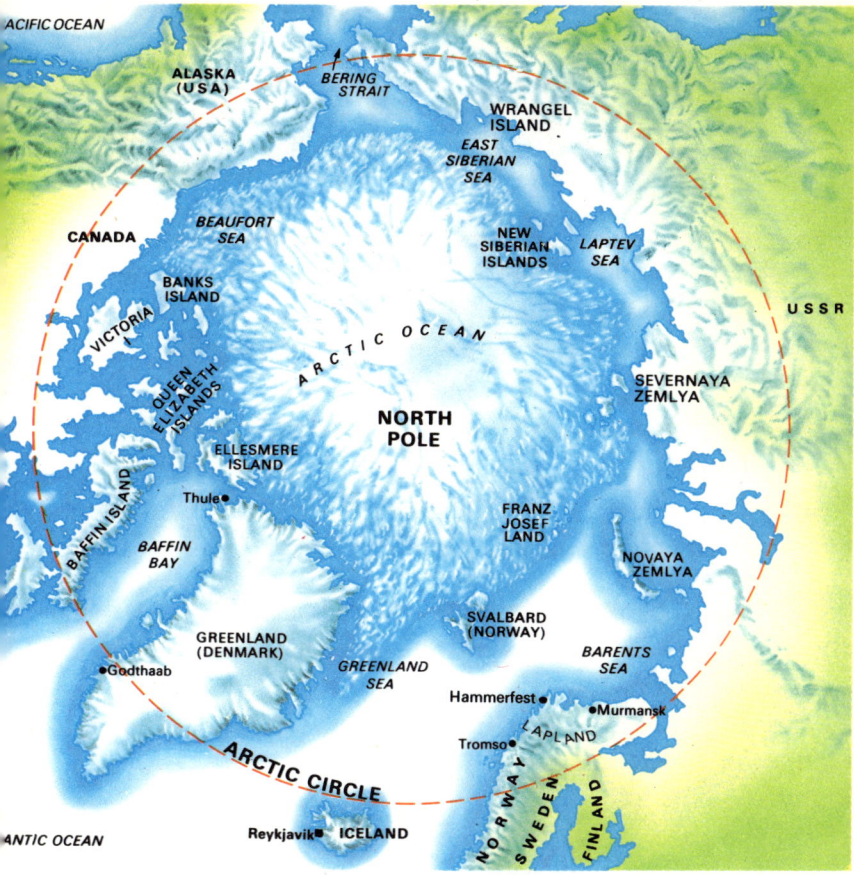

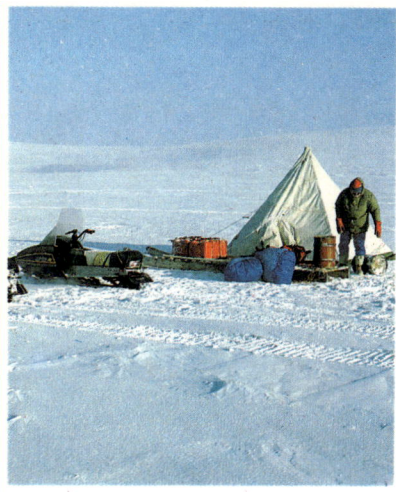

Above: A Polar Eskimo on a hunting expedition. Snowmobiles are often used now, instead of the traditional dog teams.

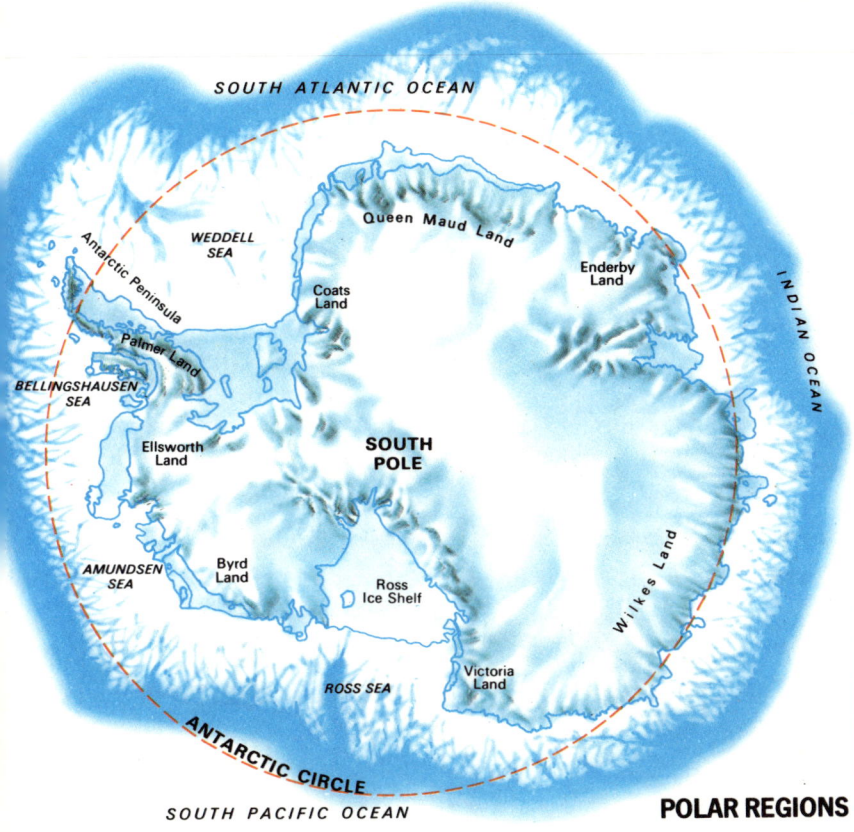

Antarctic Map (South Polar Region)

SOUTH ATLANTIC OCEAN

Antarctic Peninsula

WEDDELL SEA

Queen Maud Land

Enderby Land

Coats Land

Palmer Land

INDIAN OCEAN

BELLINGSHAUSEN SEA

Ellsworth Land

SOUTH POLE

AMUNDSEN SEA

Byrd Land

Ross Ice Shelf

Wilkes Land

Victoria Land

ROSS SEA

ANTARCTIC CIRCLE

SOUTH PACIFIC OCEAN

POLAR REGIONS

Above: The Arctic tern could be considered to be the world's migration champion. It breeds on seacoasts along the Arctic Ocean, and in August each year migrates to the Antarctic, at the other end of the world.

61

FACTS AND FIGURES

AFRICA

ALGERIA Republic of North Africa.
Area: 2,382,000 sq. km (919,600 sq. mi.).
Population: 25,000,000.
Capital: Algiers.

ANGOLA Republic of west-central Africa.
Area: 1,247,000 sq. km (481,000 sq. mi.).
Population: 8,970,000.
Capital: Luanda.

ASCENSION Island in the South Atlantic, 800 km (500 miles) south of the Equator, a dependency of St Helena.
Area: 88 sq. km (34 sq. mi).
Population: 1000.
Capital: Georgetown.

BENIN Republic on the Gulf of Guinea, West Africa.
Area: 112,600 sq. km (43,480 sq. mi.).
Population: 4,550,000.
Capital: Porto Novo.

BOTSWANA Republic of Southern Africa, a member of the Commonwealth.
Area: 600,400 sq. km (232,000 sq. mi.).
Population: 1,200,000.
Capital: Gaborone.

BURKINA FASO Republic of West Africa formerly called Upper Volta.
Area: 274,200 sq. km (105,900 sq. mi.).
Population: 7,700,000.
Capital: Ouagadougou.

BURUNDI Republic of Central Africa.
Area: 27,800 sq. km (10,750 sq. mi.).
Population: 5,200,000.
Capital: Bujumbura.

CAMEROON Republic of West Africa.
Area: 475,450 sq. km (183,580 sq. mi.).
Population: 10,870,000.
Capital: Yaoundé.

CAPE VERDE Republic, a number of islands in the North Atlantic.
Area: 4030 sq. km (1560 sq. mi.).
Population: 318,000.
Capital: Praia.

CENTRAL AFRICAN REPUBLIC Republic of Equatorial Africa within the French Community.
Area: 622,984 sq. km (240,550 sq. mi.).
Population: 3,000,000.
Capital: Bangui.

CHAD Republic of Equatorial Africa within the French Community.
Area: 1,284,000 sq. km (496,000 sq. mi.).
Population: 5,700,000.
Capital: N'djamena.

COMOROS Island republic in Indian Ocean off Mozambique, Africa.
Area: 2170 sq. km (838 sq. mi.).
Population: 460,000.
Capital: Moroni.

CONGO Republic of Equatorial Africa within the French Community.
Area: 342,000 sq. km (132,000 sq. mi.).
Population: 2,030,000.
Capital: Brazzaville.

DJIBOUTI Republic of north-east Africa within the French Community, on the Red Sea.
Area: 22,000 sq. km (8500 sq. mi.).
Population: 330,000.
Capital: Djibouti.

EGYPT Arab republic of north-east Africa.
Area: 1,000,000 sq. km (387,000 sq. mi.).
Population: 54,800,000.
Capital: Cairo.

EQUATORIAL GUINEA
Republic of West Africa.
Area: 28,000 sq. km
(10,800 sq. mi.).
Population: 390,000.
Capital: Malabo.

ETHIOPIA Republic of north-east Africa.
Area: 1,222,000 sq. km
(472,000 sq. mi.).
Population: 43,900,000.
Capital: Addis Ababa.

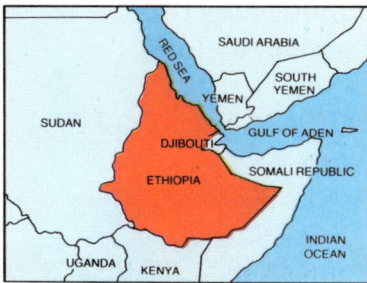

GABON Republic of Equatorial Africa within the French Community.
Area: 268,000 sq. km
(103,000 sq. mi.).
Population: 1,100,000.
Capital: Libreville.

GAMBIA Republic within the Commonwealth in West Africa.
Area: 11,300 sq. km
(4300 sq. mi.).
Population: 840,000.
Capital: Banjul.

GHANA Republic of West Africa, a member of the Commonwealth.
Area: 239,000 sq. km
(92,000 sq. mi.).
Population: 13,700,000.
Capital: Accra.

GUINEA Republic of West Africa.
Area: 246,000 sq. km
(95,000 sq. mi.).
Population: 6,150,000.
Capital: Conakry.

GUINEA-BISSAU Republic of West Africa which includes the Bijagós Islands.
Area: 36,000 sq. km
(14,000 sq. mi.).
Population: 930,000.
Capital: Bissau.

IVORY COAST Republic of West Africa.
Area: 322,500 sq. km
(124,000 sq. mi.).
Population: 11,800,000.
Capital: Abidjan.

KENYA Republic of East Africa, a member of the Commonwealth.
Area: 582,700 sq. km
(225,000 sq. mi.).
Population: 23,700,000.
Capital: Nairobi.

LESOTHO Kingdom of Southern Africa surrounded by the country of South Africa.
Area: 30,360 sq. km
(11,700 sq. mi.).
Population: 1,700,000.
Capital: Maseru.

LIBERIA Republic of West Africa.
Area: 98,938 sq. km
(38,200 sq. mi.).
Population: 2,500,000.
Capital: Monrovia.

LIBYA Republic of North Africa.
Area: 1,760,000 sq. km
(680,000 sq. mi.).
Population: 4,300,000.
Capital: Tripoli.

MADAGASCAR An island republic in Indian Ocean about 400 km (250 miles) east of Africa.
Area: 587,000 sq. km
(226,700 sq. mi.).
Population: 11,100,000.
Capital: Antananarivo.

MALAWI Republic of Southern Africa lying on the western shore of Lake Nyasa.
Area: 118,500 sq. km
(45,800 sq. mi.).
Population: 8,000,000.
Capital: Lilongwe.

MALI Republic of north-west Africa.
Area: 1,240,000 sq. km
(479,000 sq. mi.).
Population: 7,900,000.
Capital: Bamako.

MAURITANIA Republic of north-west Africa.
Area: 1,030,700 sq. km (400,000 sq. mi.).
Population: 1,800,000.
Capital: Nouakchott.

MAURITIUS An independent state in the Indian Ocean, made up of two main islands. A member of the Commonwealth.
Area: 2050 sq. km (790 sq. mi.).
Population: 1,000,000.
Capital: Port Louis.

MAYOTTE A French territory, an island in the Comoro Archipelago.
Area: 374 sq. km (145 sq. mi.).
Population: 77,000.
Capital: Dzaoudzi.

MOROCCO A monarchy of north-west Africa.
Area: 446,500 sq. km (172,400 sq. mi.).
Population: 25,400,000.
Capital: Rabat.

MOZAMBIQUE Republic of south-east Africa.
Area: 800,310 sq. km (309,000 sq. mi.).
Population: 15,300,000.
Capital: Maputo.

NAMIBIA Republic in south-west Africa which became independent in 1990. Prior to this, Namibia's status had been in dispute. South Africa claimed control as it had been granted a mandate to govern the country after World War I

by the League of Nations. However, the United Nations voted to end the mandate in 1966.
Area: 824,000 sq. km (318,000 sq. mi.).
Population: 1,200,000.
Capital: Windhoek.

NIGER Republic of West Africa.
Area: 1,267,000 sq. km (489,000 sq. mi.).
Population: 7,400,000.
Capital: Niamey.

NIGERIA Republic of West Africa.
Area: 923,000 sq. km (356,700 sq. mi.).
Population: 115,200,000.
Capital: Lagos (Abuja).

RÉUNION A French overseas department in the Indian Ocean.
Area: 2500 sq. km (969 sq. mi.).
Population: 575,000.
Capital: St Denis.

RWANDA Republic of Central Africa.
Area: 26,400 sq. km. (10,000 sq. mi.).
Population: 7,300,000.
Capital: Kigali.

ST HELENA British colony, including the island of Ascension and the four islands of Tristan da Cunha, in the South Atlantic.
St Helena **area:** 122 sq. km (47 sq. mi.).
Population: 5,200.
Capital: Jamestown.

SÃO TOMÉ AND PRINCIPE Island republic off the west coast of Africa.
Area: 964 sq. km (372 sq. mi.).
Population: 114,000.
Capital: São Tomé.

SENEGAL Republic of West Africa.
Area: 196,000 sq. km (76,000 sq. mi.).
Population: 7,700,000.
Capital: Dakar.

SEYCHELLES Island republic of the Indian Ocean, a member of the Commonwealth.
Area: 443 sq. km (171 sq. mi.).
Population: 70,000.
Capital: Victoria.

SIERRA LEONE Republic of West Africa, an independent member of the Commonwealth.
Area: 71,700 sq. km (27,700 sq. mi.).
Population: 4,300,000.
Capital: Freetown.

SOMALI REPUBLIC Republic of Africa, facing Aden.
Area: 637,700 sq. km (246,000 sq. mi.).
Population: 8,600,000.
Capital: Mogadishu.

SOUTH AFRICA Republic of Southern Africa.
Area: 1,221,000 sq. km (471,500 sq. mi.).
Population: 35,600,000.
Capital: Cape Town (seat of Legislature or law-making assembly); Pretoria (seat of Government); Bloemfontein (judicial capital).

SUDAN Republic of north-east Africa.
Area: 2,506,000 sq. km (967,500 sq. mi.).
Population: 25,000,000.
Capital: Khartoum.

SWAZILAND Kingdom of Southern Africa, a member of the Commonwealth.
Area: 17,400 sq. km (6,700 sq. mi.).
Population: 760,000.
Capital: Mbabane.

TANZANIA Republic of East Africa, a member of the Commonwealth.
Area: 945,000 sq. km (365,000 sq. mi.).
Population: 24,700,000.
Capital: Dodoma.

TOGO Republic of West Africa.
Area: 56,000 sq. km (21,600 sq. mi.).
Population: 3,400,000.
Capital: Lomé.

TRISTAN DA CUNHA Island in the South Atlantic Ocean, a dependency of St Helena.
Area: 98 sq. km (38 sq. mi.).
Population: 320.
Capital: Edinburgh.

TUNISIA Republic of North Africa.
Area: 163,000 sq. km (63,000 sq. mi.).
Population: 7,900,000.
Capital: Tunis.

UGANDA Republic of east-central Africa. A member of the Commonwealth.
Area: 236,000 sq. km (91,000 sq. mi.).
Population: 16,800,000.
Capital: Kampala.

WESTERN SAHARA A North African territory claimed by Morocco and local nationalists.
Area: 266,000 sq. km (102,700 sq. mi.).
Population: 179,000.
Capital: El Aiun.

ZAIRE Republic of west-central Africa.
Area: 2,345,400 sq. km (905,600 sq. mi.).
Population: 34,000,000.
Capital: Kinshasa.

ZAMBIA Republic in south-central Africa. A member of the Commonwealth.
Area: 752,600 sq. km (290,600 sq. mi.).
Population: 7,800,000.
Capital: Lusaka.

ZIMBABWE Republic of Southern Africa. A member of the Commonwealth.
Area: 390,600 sq. km (150,800 sq. mi.).
Population: 10,000,000.
Capital: Harare.

ASIA

AFGHANISTAN Republic of south-western Asia.
Area: 650,000 sq. km (250,000 sq. mi.).
Population: 16,600,000.
Capital: Kabul.

BAHRAIN Island group off Saudi Arabia forming a state.
Area: 622 sq. km (240 sq. mi.).
Population: 480,000.
Capital: Manama.

BANGLADESH Republic in south-east Asia. A member of the Commonwealth.
Area: 144,000 sq. km (55,600 sq. mi.).
Population: 113,000,000.
Capital: Dacca.

BHUTAN Kingdom of the Himalayas.
Area: 47,000 sq. km (18,000 sq. mi.).
Population: 1,500,000.
Capital: Thimphu.

BRUNEI Sultanate of Borneo. Commonwealth member.
Area: 5,760 sq. km (2,230 sq. mi.).
Population: 240,000.
Capital: Bandar Seri Begawan.

CAMBODIA (Kampuchea)
Republic of south-east Asia.
Area: 181,000 sq. km
(70,000 sq. mi.).
Population: 6,900,000.
Capital: Phnom Penh.

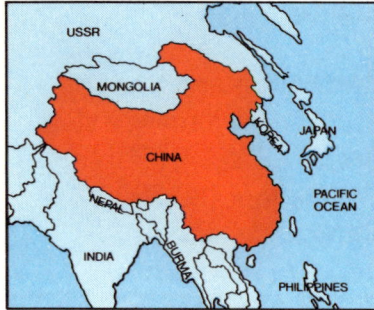

CHINA
Republic of east Asia.
Area: 9,597,000 sq. km
(3,706,000 sq. mi.).
Population: 1,070,600,000.
Capital: Beijing (Peking).

HONG KONG
British dependency on the south coast of China.
Area: 1061 sq. km (410
sq. mi.).
Population: 5,423,000.
Capital: Victoria, usually called Hong Kong.

INDIA
Republic of Asia. A member of the Commonwealth.
Area: 3,287,590 sq. km
(1,269,345 sq. mi.).
Population: 833,400,000.
Capital: New Delhi.

INDONESIA
Republic of south-east Asia.
Area: 1,903,650 sq. km
(735,003 sq. mi.).
Population: 187,700,000.
Capital: Djakarta.

IRAN
Islamic Republic of south-west Asia. It is one of the Gulf States.
Area: 1,648,000 sq. km.
(636,296 sq. mi.).
Population: 51,000,000.
Capital: Tehran.

IRAQ
Republic of south-west Asia.
Area: 435,000 sq. km
(168,000 sq. mi.).
Population: 17,600,000.
Capital: Baghdad.

ISRAEL
Republic of the Middle East.
Area: 20,700 sq. km
(8000 sq. mi.).
Population: 4,500,000.
Capital: Jerusalem.

JAPAN
Constitutional monarchy of the Far East.
Area: 372,300 sq. km
(143,800 sq. mi.).
Population: 123,200,000.
Capital: Tokyo.

JORDAN
Kingdom of the Middle East.
Area: 97,740 sq. km
(37,700 sq. mi.).
Population: 3,000,000.
Capital: Amman.

KOREA, NORTH
Republic of the Far East bordering on north-east China.
Area: 120,500 sq. km
(46,500 sq. mi.).
Population: 22,000,000.
Capital: Pyongyang.

KOREA, SOUTH
Republic of the Far East.
Area: 98,000 sq. km
(38,000 sq. mi.).
Population: 45,200,000.
Capital: Seoul.

KUWAIT
An Emirate on the Persian Gulf in south-west Asia.
Area: 17,800 sq. km
(6900 sq. mi.).
Population: 2,000,000.
Capital: Kuwait.

LAOS
Republic of south-east Asia lying in the Mekong Basin.
Area: 236,800 sq. km
(91,400 sq. mi.).
Population: 3,900,000.
Capital: Vientiane.

LEBANON
Republic of the Middle East at the eastern end of the Mediterranean Sea.
Area: 10,400 sq. km
(4000 sq. mi.).
Population: 2,900,000.
Capital: Beirut.

MACÃO An overseas territory of Portugal on the south-east coast of China.
Area: 16 sq. km (6 sq. mi.).
Population: 430,000.
Capital: Macão.

MALAYSIA A state of south-east Asia. A member of the Commonwealth.
Area: 330,000 sq. km (127,300 sq. mi.).
Population: 16,900,000.
Capital: Kuala Lumpur.

MALDIVES An island republic of the Indian Ocean southwest of India, with about 2000 islands. A member of the Commonwealth.
Area: 300 sq. km (115 sq. mi.).
Population: 200,000.
Capital: Malé.

MONGOLIA Republic of central Asia.
Area: 1,565,000 sq. km (604,300 sq. mi.).
Population: 2,000,000.
Capital: Ulan Bator.

MYANMAR (Burma) Republic of south-east Asia.
Area: 676,500 sq. km (261,230 sq. mi.).
Population: 40,000,000.
Capital: Yangon (Rangoon).

NEPAL A monarchy of the Himalayas between China and India.
Area: 140,800 sq. km (54,000 sq. mi.).
Population: 18,800,000.
Capital: Katmandu.

OMAN A sultanate at the eastern end of the Arabian peninsula, bordering the Arabian Sea.
Area: 212,400 sq. km (82,000 sq. mi.).
Population: 1,400,000.
Capital: Muscat.

PAKISTAN Republic of southern Asia. Member of the Commonwealth.
Area: 804,000 sq. km (310,400 sq. mi.).
Population: 110,400,000.
Capital: Islamabad.

PHILIPPINES Republic of many islands in south-east Asia.
Area: 330,000 sq. km (116,000 sq. mi.).
Population: 62,000,000.
Capital: Manila.

QATAR An Emirate, a peninsula in the Persian Gulf.
Area: 11,000 sq. km (4000 sq. mi.).
Population: 340,000.
Capital: Doha.

SAUDI ARABIA Kingdom of the Arabian peninsula.
Area: 2,175,600 sq. km (840,000 sq. mi.).
Population: 12,700,000.
Capital: Riyadh.

SINGAPORE Island republic at tip of the Malaya peninsula, a member of the Commonwealth.
Area: 580 sq. km (224 sq. mi.).
Population: 2,700,000.
Capital: Singapore.

SRI LANKA Island republic of south Asia in the Indian Ocean, a member of the Commonwealth.
Area: 65,600 sq. km (25,000 sq. mi.).
Population: 17,500,000.
Capital: Colombo.

SYRIA Republic of the Middle East.
Area: 185,000 sq. km (71,500 sq. mi.).
Population: 12,200,000.
Capital: Damascus.

TAIWAN (Republic of China). Republic about 140 km (90 miles) off mainland China.
Area: 36,000 sq. km (14,000 sq. mi.).
Population: 20,300,000.
Capital: Taipei.

THAILAND Kingdom of south-east Asia.
Area: 514,000 sq. km (198,000 sq. mi.).
Population: 55,000,000.
Capital: Bangkok.

TURKEY Republic partly in Europe, partly in Asia.
Area: 780,000 sq. km (301,400 sq. mi.).
Population: 55,400,000.
Capital: Ankara.

UNITED ARAB EMIRATES A federation of seven independent emirates in the Persian Gulf. They are: Abu Dhabi, Ajman, Dubai, Fujairah, Ras al Khaimah, Sharjah and Umm al Qaiwain.
Area: 83,600 sq. km (32,300 sq. mi.).
Population: 1,500,000.
Capital: Abu Dhabi.

VIETNAM Republic of southeast Asia bordering on south China.
Area: 330,000 sq. km (127,250 sq. mi.).
Population: 66,700,000.
Capital: Hanoi.

YEMEN Republic in the Arabian peninsula.
Area: 528,000 sq.km (211,200 sq.mi.).
Population: 9,274,000.
Capital: San'a.

EUROPE

ALBANIA Republic of Europe in the Balkans.
Area: 28,700 sq. km (11,100 sq. mi.).
Population: 3,200,000.
Capital: Tirana.

ANDORRA Tiny landlocked country of the Pyrenees: sovereignty divided between France and the Spanish Bishop of Urgel.
Area: 453 sq. km (175 sq. mi.).
Population: 56,000.
Capital: Andorra la Vella.

AUSTRIA Republic of central Europe.
Area: 83,850 sq. km (32,376 sq. mi.).
Population: 7,500,000.
Capital: Vienna.

BELGIUM Kingdom of northern Europe.
Area: 30,500 sq. km (11,800 sq. mi.).
Population: 9,900,000.
Capital: Brussels.

BULGARIA Republic of Europe in the Balkans.
Area: 111,000 sq. km (42,855 sq. mi.).
Population: 9,000,000.
Capital: Sofia.

CYPRUS Island republic in the Mediterranean, divided since Turkish forces occupied the North in 1974. A member of the Commonwealth.
Area: 9,250 sq. km (3600 sq. mi.).
Population: 700,000.
Capital: Nicosia.

CZECHOSLOVAKIA Republic of central Europe.
Area: 128,000 sq. km (50,000 sq. mi.).
Population: 15,500,000.
Capital: Prague.

DENMARK Kingdom of northern Europe.
Area: 45,000 sq. km (17,400 sq. mi.).
Population: 5,100,000.
Capital: Copenhagen.

FINLAND Republic of northeast Europe
Area: 337,000 sq. km (130,000 sq. mi.).
Population: 5,000,000.
Capital: Helsinki.

FRANCE Republic of western Europe.
Area: 547,000 sq. km (213,000 sq. mi.).
Population: 55,800,000.
Capital: Paris.

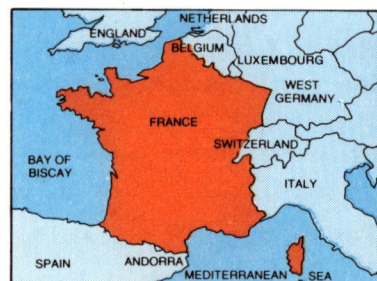

GERMANY
Area: 356,755 sq. km (142,702 sq. mi.).
Population: 78,270,000.
Capital: Berlin.

GIBRALTAR British colony at tip of Spain.
Area: 6.5 sq. km (2½ sq. mi.).
Population: 31,000.
Capital: Gibraltar.

GREECE Republic of south-east Europe which includes many islands.
Area: 132,000 sq. km (51,000 sq. mi.).
Population: 10,100,000.
Capital: Athens.

GREENLAND Self-governing part of Denmark in the North Atlantic.
Area: 2,176,000 sq. km (840,000 sq. mi.).
Population: 54,000.
Capital: Godthaab.

HUNGARY Republic of central Europe.
Area: 93,000 sq. km (36,000 sq. mi.).
Population: 10,500,000.
Capital: Budapest.

ICELAND Island republic of the northern Atlantic.
Area: 103,000 sq. km (40,000 sq. mi.).
Population: 244,000.
Capital: Reykjavik.

IRELAND, REPUBLIC OF Republic of northern Europe.
Area: 70,200 sq. km (27,000 sq. mi.).
Population: 3,700,000.
Capital: Dublin.

ITALY Republic of southern Europe.
Area: 301,000 sq. km (116,000 sq. mi.).
Population: 57,400,000.
Capital: Rome.

LIECHTENSTEIN A principality of western Europe.
Area: 157 sq. km (62 sq. mi.).
Population: 28,000.
Capital: Vaduz.

LUXEMBOURG A Grand Duchy of western Europe.
Area: 2600 sq. km (1000 sq. mi.).
Population: 400,000.
Capital: Luxembourg City.

MALTA An island republic of the Mediterranean, a member of the Commonwealth.
Area: 316 sq. km (122 sq. mi.).
Population: 400,000.
Capital: Valetta.

MONACO A principality on the Mediterranean coast, in south-east France.
Area: 1.9 sq. km (467 acres).
Population: 28,000.
Capital: Monaco.

NETHERLANDS Kingdom of north-west Europe.
Area: 40,844 sq. km (15,770 sq. mi.).
Population: 14,700,000.
Capital: Amsterdam.

NORWAY Kingdom of northern Europe.
Area: 324,219 sq. km (125,182 sq. mi.).
Population: 4,200,000.
Capital: Oslo.

POLAND Republic of eastern Europe.
Area: 312,677 sq. km (120,725 sq. mi.).
Population: 38,400,000.
Capital: Warsaw.

FACTS AND FIGURES

PORTUGAL Republic in south-west Europe.
Area: 92,082 sq. km (35,553 sq. mi.).
Population: 10,240,000.
Capital: Lisbon.

ROMANIA Republic in eastern Europe.
Area: 237,500 sq. km (91,699 sq. mi.).
Population: 22,316,000.
Capital: Bucharest.

RUSSIA AND THE FORMER REPUBLICS OF THE USSR
Russia is the world's largest nation, spanning Europe and Asia.
Total Area: 22,402,200 sq. km (8,650,000 sq. mi.).
Population: 287,015,000.
Capital: Moscow.
Former Republics of the USSR: Armenia; Azerbaijan; Belorussia; Georgia; Kazakhstan; Kirghizia; Moldavia; Tadzhikistan; Turkmenistan; Ukraine; and Uzbekistan. Estonia, Latvia, and Lithuania were also former Republics of the USSR, but are now recognized as independent nations.

SAN MARINO Republic in the Apennines, Italy.
Area: 61 sq. km (24 sq. mi.).
Population: 23,000.
Capital: San Marino.

SPAIN Kingdom of Europe.
Area: 504,700 sq. km (195,000 sq. mi.).
Population: 39,800,000.
Capital: Madrid.

SWEDEN Kingdom of northern Europe.
Area: 450,000 sq. km (173,700 sq. mi.).
Population: 8,300,000.
Capital: Stockholm.

SWITZERLAND Republic of western Europe.
Area: 41,000 sq. km (16,000 sq. mi.).
Population: 6,500,000.
Capital: Bern.

UNITED KINGDOM Kingdom of north-west Europe.
Area: 244,046 sq. km (94,232 sq. mi.).
Population: 56,800,000.
Capital: London.
The UK consists of:
England
Area: 130,363 sq. km (50,336 sq. mi.).
Population: 47,250,000.
Capital: London.
Scotland
Area: 78,772 sq. km (30,416 sq. mi.).
Population: 5,120,000.
Capital: Edinburgh.
Wales
Area: 20,763 sq. km (8017 sq. mi.).
Population: 2,820,000.
Capital: Cardiff.

Northern Ireland
Area: 14,148 sq. km (5463 sq. mi.).
Population: 1,600,000.
Capital: Belfast.

Isle of Man
Area: 588 sq. km (227 sq. mi.).
Population: 62,000.
Capital: Douglas.

Channel Islands Group of islands off north-west coast of France.
Area: 195 sq. km (75 sq. mi.).
Jersey
Area: 116 sq. km (45 sq. mi.).
Population: 73,000.
Capital: St. Helier.
Guernsey
Area: 63 sq. km ($24\frac{1}{2}$ sq. mi.).
Area of 6 Dependencies: 16 sq. km (5 sq. mi.).
Total population: 131,000.
Capital: St. Peter Port.

VATICAN CITY State in north-west Rome, Italy, in which is located the government of the Roman Catholic Church.
Area: 44 hectares (108.7 acres).
Population: 1000.

YUGOSLAVIA A country in south-east Europe.
Total Area: 255,800 sq. km (98,800 sq. mi.).
Population: 23,898,000.
Capital: Belgrade.
In 1991, the republics of Slovenia and Croatia declared their independence. They have been recognized by the EC (1992). However, fighting between Croats and Serbs continued into 1992.

NORTH AND CENTRAL AMERICA

ANGUILLA British colony of the Leeward Islands, West Indies.
Area: 90 sq. km (35 sq. mi.).
Population: 6,500.
Capital: The Valley.

ANTIGUA and BARBUDA State of the West Indies within the Commonwealth.
Area: 440 sq. km (170 sq. mi.).
Population: 82,000.
Capital: St. John's.

BAHAMAS An independent Commonwealth member in the West Atlantic.
Area: 14,000 sq. km (5,380 sq. mi.).
Population: 240,000.
Capital: Nassau.

BARBADOS Independent Commonwealth member in the West Indies.
Area: 430 sq. km (166 sq. mi.).
Population: 250,000.
Capital: Bridgetown.

BELIZE State on the east coast of Central America, a member of the Commonwealth.
Area: 22,960 sq. km (8860 sq. mi.).
Population: 180,000.
Capital: Belmopan.

BERMUDA British dependent territory in the West Atlantic.
Area: 53 sq. km (20 sq. mi.).
Population: 62,000.
Capital: Hamilton.

CANADA Independent member of the Commonwealth in the north of North America.
Area: 9,976,000 sq. km (3,852,000 sq. mi.).
Population: 25,600,000.
Capital: Ottawa.
Canada has 12 provinces listed below:

Canada

Province	Capital
Alberta	Edmonton
British Columbia	Victoria
Manitoba	Winnipeg
New Brunswick	Fredericton
Newfoundland	St. John's
Northwest Terr.	Yellowknife
Nova Scotia	Halifax
Ontario	Toronto
Prince Edward Is.	Charlottetown
Quebec	Quebec
Saskatchewan	Regina
Yukon Territory	Whitehorse

CAYMAN ISLANDS British colony, a number of islands in the West Indies.
Area: 260 sq. km (100 sq. mi.).
Population: 23,000.
Capital: George Town.

COSTA RICA Republic of Central America.
Area: 50,700 sq. km (19,600 sq. mi.).
Population: 2,900,000.
Capital: San José.

CUBA West Indian republic.
Area: 114,500 sq. km (44,220 sq. mi.).
Population: 10,600,000.
Capital: Havana.

DOMINICA Republic within the Commonwealth in the Windward Islands, West Indies
Area: 751 sq. km (290 sq. mi.).
Population: 74,000.
Capital: Roseau.

DOMINICAN REPUBLIC Republic of the West Indies, occupying two-thirds of the island of Hispaniola.
Area: 49,000 sq. km (18,800 sq. mi.).
Population: 7,300,000.
Capital: Santo Domingo.

EL SALVADOR Republic of Central America.
Area: 21,000 sq. km (8000 sq. mi.).
Population: 5,550,000.
Capital: San Salvador.

GRENADA An independent country within the Commonwealth, one of the Windward Islands.
Area: 344 sq. km (133 sq. mi.).
Population: 86,000.
Capital: St. George's.

GUADELOUPE A French overseas department in the West Indies.
Area: 1780 sq. km (688 sq. mi.).
Population: 332,000.
Capital: Basse-Terre.

GUATEMALA Republic of Central America.
Area: 108,900 sq. km (42,000 sq. mi.).
Population: 9,400,000.
Capital: Guatemala City.

HAITI Republic of the West Indies, occupying one third of the island of Hispaniola.
Area: 28,000 sq. km (10,700 sq. mi.).
Population: 6,200,000.
Capital: Port-au-Prince.

HONDURAS Republic of Central America.
Area: 112,000 sq. km. (43,000 sq. mi.).
Population: 5,100,000.
Capital: Tegucigalpa.

JAMAICA An independent member of the Commonwealth in the West Indies.
Area: 11,000 sq. km (4,200 sq. mi.).
Population: 2,400,000.
Capital: Kingston.

MARTINIQUE A French overseas department in the West Indies.
Area: 1,100 sq. km (426 sq. mi.).
Population: 117,000.
Capital: Fort-de-France.

MEXICO Republic of North America.
Area: 1,970,000 sq. km (761,000 sq. mi.).
Population: 88,000,000.
Capital: Mexico City.

MONTSERRAT British colony in the Leeward Islands, West Indies.
Area: 98 sq. km (38 sq. mi.).
Population: 12,000.
Capital: Plymouth.

NETHERLANDS ANTILLES (Dutch West Indies) Two groups of Dutch islands in the Caribbean, with full internal autonomy.
Area: 960 sq. km (370 sq. mi.).
Population: 187,000.
Capital: Willemstad.

NICARAGUA Republic of Central America.
Area: 130,000 sq. km (50,000 sq. mi.).
Population: 3,700,000.
Capital: Managua.

PANAMA Republic of Central America.
Area: 75,700 sq. km (29,000 sq. mi.).
Population: 2,400,000.
Capital: Panama.

PUERTO RICO A United States self-governing Commonwealth in the West Indies.
Area: 8900 sq. km (3435 sq. mi.).
Population: 3,666,000.
Capital: San Juan.

ST KITTS-NEVIS A state in the Leeward Islands of the West Indies within the Commonwealth.
Area: 260 sq. km (100 sq. mi.).
Population: 40,000.
Capital: Basseterre.

ST LUCIA An independent state within the Commonwealth; one of the Windward Islands.
Area: 616 sq. km (238 sq. mi.).
Population: 120,000.
Capital: Castries.

ST PIERRE AND MIQUELON A French overseas department; eight islands off Newfoundland, Canada.
Area: 242 sq. km (93 sq. mi.).
Population: 6000.
Capital: St. Pierre.

ST VINCENT AND THE GRENADINES An independent member of the Commonwealth in the Windward Islands, West Indies.
Area: 388 sq. km (150 sq. mi.).

Population: 100,000.
Capital: Kingstown.

TRINIDAD AND TOBAGO
Island Republic of the West Indies within the Commonwealth.
Area: 5000 sq. km (2000 sq. mi.).
Population: 1,300,000.
Capital: Port-of-Spain.

TURKS AND CAICOS ISLANDS
British colony in the Caribbean.
Area: 430 sq. km (166 sq. mi.).
Population: 7,200.
Capital: Cockburn Town.

UNITED STATES OF AMERICA
Federal republic of North America.
Area: 9,363,123 sq. km (3,615,319 sq. mi.).
Population: 249,800,000.
Capital: Washington, District of Columbia. The United States is made up of 50 states. These are listed below:

State	Capital
Alabama	Montgomery
Alaska	Juneau
Arizona	Phoenix
Arkansas	Little Rock
California	Sacramento
Colorado	Denver
Connecticut	Hartford
Delaware	Dover
Florida	Tallahassee
Georgia	Atlanta
Hawaii	Honolulu
Idaho	Boise
Illinois	Springfield
Indiana	Indianapolis
Iowa	Des Moines
Kansas	Topeka
Kentucky	Frankfort
Louisiana	Baton Rouge
Maine	Augusta
Maryland	Annapolis
Massachusetts	Boston
Michigan	Lansing
Minnesota	St. Paul
Mississippi	Jackson
Missouri	Jefferson City
Montana	Helena
Nebraska	Lincoln
Nevada	Carson City
New Hampshire	Concord
New Jersey	Trenton
New Mexico	Santa Fé
New York	Albany
North Carolina	Raleigh
North Dakota	Bismarck
Ohio	Columbus
Oklahoma	Oklahoma City
Oregon	Salem
Pennsylvania	Harrisburg
Rhode Island	Providence
South Carolina	Columbia
South Dakota	Pierre
Tennessee	Nashville
Texas	Austin
Utah	Salt Lake City
Vermont	Montpelier
Virginia	Richmond
Washington	Olympia
West Virginia	Charlestown
Wisconsin	Madison
Wyoming	Cheyenne

VIRGIN ISLANDS (British)
Group of 36, West Indies.
Area: 153 sq. km (59 sq. mi.).
Population: 11,500.
Capital: Road Town.

VIRGIN ISLANDS (US)
A territory near Puerto Rico in the West Indies.
Area: 344 sq. km (133 sq. mi.).
Population: 119,000.
Capital: Charlotte Amalie.

SOUTH AMERICA

ARGENTINA Republic lying on the east coast of South America.
Area: 2,766,890 sq. km (1,068,360 sq. mi.).
Population: 32,600,000.
Capital: Buenos Aires.

BOLIVIA Landlocked republic at the centre of South America.
Area: 1,093,500 sq. km (424,000 sq. mi.).
Population: 6,900,000.
Capital: La Paz (seat of government); Sucre (legal capital).

BRAZIL Republic, largest country of South America in both area and population.
Area: 8,512,000 sq. km (3,286,670 sq. mi.).
Population: 154,000,000.
Capital: Brasilia.

CHILE Republic lying on the western coast of South America.
Area: 757,000 sq. km (292,274, sq. mi.).
Population: 12,900,000.
Capital: Santiago.

COLOMBIA Republic of South America.
Area: 1,139,000 sq. km (440,000 sq. mi.).
Population: 31,800,000.
Capital: Bogota.

ECUADOR Republic of South America.
Area: 283,600 sq. km (109,500 sq. mi.).
Population: 10,500,000.
Capital: Quito.

FALKLAND ISLANDS British colony in the South Atlantic.
Area: 12,200 sq. km (4700 sq. mi.).
Population: 2000.
Capital: Stanley.

FRENCH GUIANA A French overseas department in north-east South America.
Area: 91,000 sq. km (35,000 sq. mi.).
Population: 92,000.
Capital: Cayenne.

GUYANA Republic of north-east South America, a member of the Commonwealth.
Area: 215,000 sq. km (83,000 sq. mi.).
Population: 770,000.
Capital: Georgetown.

PARAGUAY Landlocked republic at the centre of South America.
Area: 406,700 sq. km (157,000 sq. mi.).
Population: 4,500,000.
Capital: Asunción.

PERU Republic lying on the western coast of South America.
Area: 1,285,000 sq. km (496,000 sq. mi.).
Population: 21,800,000.
Capital: Lima.

SURINAM Small republic of the north-east coast of South America.
Area: 163,300 sq. km (63,000 sq. mi.).
Population: 380,000.
Capital: Paramaribo.

URUGUAY Republic of South America.
Area: 176,200 sq. km (68,000 sq. mi.).
Population: 3,000,000.
Capital: Montevideo.

VENEZUELA Republic of South America.
Area: 912,000 sq. km (352,000 sq. mi.).
Population: 19,200,000.
Capital: Caracas.

OCEANIA

AUSTRALIA An independent Commonwealth member, occupying the continent of Australia and outlying islands.
Area: 7,686,800 sq. km (2,968,000 sq. mi.).
Population: 16,100,000.
Capital: Canberra.
States and territories include:

Australian Capital Territory
New South Wales
Northern Territory   Queensland
South Australia   Tasmania
Western Australia   Victoria.

COOK ISLANDS Self-governing territory of New Zealand in the South Pacific.
Area: 234 sq. mi (90 sq. mi.).
Population: 18,000.
Capital: Avarua.

FIJI Republic in south-west Pacific.
Area: 18,300 sq. km (7050 sq. mi.).
Population: 700,000.
Capital: Suva.

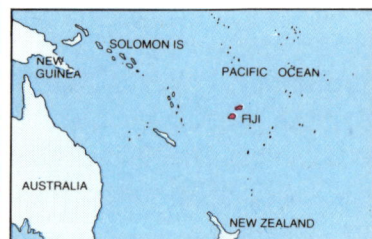

FRENCH POLYNESIA A French overseas department in the Eastern Pacific.
Area: 4000 sq. km (1550 sq. mi.).
Population: 166,000.
Capital: Papeete.

GUAM A territory of the United States in the Marianas archipelago in the North Pacific.
Area: 549 sq. km (212 sq. mi.).
Population: 99,000.
Capital: Agana.

KIRIBATI Island republic of the Central Pacific, a member of the Commonwealth.
Area: 930 sq. km (360 sq. mi.).
Population: 63,000.
Capital: Tarawa.

NAURU An island republic in the Western Pacific, with special status within the Commonwealth.
Area: 21 sq. km (8 sq. mi.).
Population: 8000.
Capital: Nauru.

NEW ZEALAND An independent member of the Commonwealth in the south-west Pacific.
Area: 268,000 sq. km (103,700 sq. mi.).
Population: 3,400,000.
Capital: Wellington.

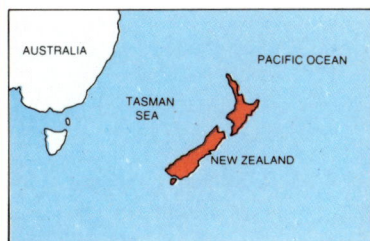

NIUE A self-governing territory of New Zealand in the Cook Islands, South Pacific.
Area: 260 sq. km (100 sq. mi.).
Population: 4000.
Capital: Alofi.

NORFOLK ISLAND An Australian territory in the south-west Pacific.
Area: 36 sq. km (14 sq. mi.).
Population: 2000.
Capital: Kingstown.

PALAU, FEDERATED STATES OF MICRONESIA, MARIANA ISLANDS AND MARSHALL ISLANDS
Formerly governed by the United States. They are now independent, except Palau which still remains under trusteeship.
Area: 1780 sq. km (687 sq. mi.).
Population: 149,000.

PAPUA NEW GUINEA An independent Commonwealth state in the south-west Pacific.
Area: 461,700 sq. km (178,200 sq. mi.).
Population: 3,600,000.
Capital: Port Moresby.

PITCAIRN ISLAND British colony in the South Pacific.
Area: 5 sq. km (2 sq. mi.).
Population: 63.
Capital: Adamstown.

SAMOA, AMERICAN Group of eight islands in the South Pacific, governed by the United States.
Area: 197 sq. km (76 sq. mi.).
Population: 35,000.
Capital: Pago Pago.

SAMOA, WESTERN An independent Commonwealth member in the Pacific.
Area: 2900 sq. km (1090 sq. mi.).
Population: 200,000.
Capital: Apia.

SOLOMON ISLANDS An independent state, a member of the Commonwealth, in the south-west Pacific.
Area: 28,500 sq. km (11,000 sq. mi.).
Population: 300,000.
Capital: Honiara.

TONGA Island kingdom in the South Pacific within the Commonwealth.
Area: 700 sq. km (270 sq. mi.).
Population: 100,000.
Capital: Nuku'alofa.

TUVALU An independent member of the Commonwealth, a group of islands in the South Pacific.
Area: 8 sq. km (3 sq. mi.).
Population: 8,500.
Capital: Fongafale.

VANUATU Island republic in the south-west Pacific, a member of the Commonwealth.
Area: 14,800 sq. km (5700 sq. mi.).
Population: 136,000.
Capital: Port Vila.

WALLIS AND FUTUNA ISLANDS A French overseas territory in the south-west Pacific.
Area: 200 sq. km (77 sq. mi.).
Population: 9000.
Capital: Mata-Uta.

MAJOR WARS

Name	Date	Won by	Against
Abyssinian War	1935–1936	Italy	Abyssinia (Ethiopia)
American War of Independence	1775–1783	Thirteen Colonies	Britain
Austrian Succession, War of the	1740–1748	Austria, Hungary, Britain, Holland	Bavaria, France, Poland, Prussia, Sardinia, Saxony, Spain
Boer (South African) War	1899–1902	Britain	Boer Republics
Chinese-Japanese Wars	1894–1895	Japan	China
	1931–1933	Japan	China
	1937–1945	China	Japan
Civil War, American	1861–1865	23 Northern States (the Union)	11 Southern States (the Confederacy)
Civil War, English	1642–1646	Parliament	Charles I
Civil War, Nigerian	1967–1970	Federal government	Biafra
Civil War, Pakistan	1971	East Pakistan (Bangladesh) and India	West Pakistan
Civil War, Spanish	1936–1939	Junta de Defensa Nacional (Fascists)	Republican government
Crimean War	1853–1856	Britain, France, Sardinia, Turkey	Russia
Franco-Prussian War	1870–1871	Prussia and other German states	France
Gulf War	1990–91	United Nations	Iraq
Hundred Years War	1337–1453	France	England
Iran-Iraq War	1980–1988	Neither side	—
Korean War	1950–1953	South Korea and United Nations forces	North Korea and Chinese forces
Mexican-American War	1846–1848	United States	Mexico
Napoleonic Wars	1792–1815	Austria, Britain, Prussia, Russia, Spain, Sweden	France
October War	1973	Ceasefire arranged by UN; fought by Israel against the Arab States of Egypt, Syria, Iraq, Sudan, Saudi Arabi, Lebanon	
Peloponnesian War	431–404 BC	Peloponnesian League – Sparta and allies	Athens
Punic Wars	264–146 BC	Rome	Carthage
Russo-Japanese War	1904–1905	Japan	Russia
Seven Years' War	1756–1763	Britain, Prussia, Hanover	Austria, France, Russia, Sweden
Seven Weeks' War	1866	Prussia, Italy	Austria, German states
Six-Day War	1967	Israel	Egypt, Syria, Jordan, Iraq
Spanish-American War	1898	United States	Spain
Spanish Succession, War of the	1701–1713	England, Austria, Prussia, the Netherlands	France, Bavaria, Cologne
Thirty Years War	1618–1648	France, Sweden, the German Protestant states	The Holy Roman Empire, Spain
Vietnam War	1957–1975	North Vietnam	South Vietnam, United States
War of 1812	1812–1814	United States	Britain
Wars of the Roses	1455–1485	House of Lancaster	House of York
World War I	1914–1918	Belgium, Britain and Empire, France, Italy, Japan, Russia, Serbia, United States	Austria-Hungary, Bulgaria, Germany, Ottoman Empire
World War II	1939–1945	Australia, Belgium, Britain, Canada, China, Denmark, France, Greece, Netherlands, New Zealand, Norway, Poland, Russia, South Africa, United States, Yugoslavia	Bulgaria, Finland, Germany, Hungary, Italy, Japan, Romania
Yom Kippur	1973	Israel	Egypt, Syria

THE UNITED NATIONS

The United Nations (UN) is an international organization that works for world peace and security, and for the betterment of mankind. More than 140 independent nations belong to the UN. Member countries send representatives to the UN headquarters in New York City. There are six major organs of the UN, which carry on the work of the organization at the headquarters. There are also a number of self-governing specialized agencies, such as the World Health Organization and the International Monetary Fund, that have a special relationship with the UN.

Principal Organs of the UN

General Assembly consists of all members, each having one vote. Most of work done in committees: (1) Political Security, (2) Economic and Financial, (3) Social, Humanitarian, and Cultural, (4) Trust and Non-Self-Governing Territories, (5) Administrative and Budgetary, (6) Legal.

Security Council consists of 15 members each with one vote. There are five permanent members – China, France, UK, USA, and USSR – the others being elected for two-year terms. Main object: maintenance of peace and security.

Economic and Social Council is responsible under General Assembly for carrying out functions of the UN with regard to international economic, social, cultural, educational, health, and related matters.

Trusteeship Council administers Trust Territories.

International Court of Justice composed of 15 judges (all different nationalities) elected by UN. Meets at The Hague.

The Secretariat is composed of the Secretary-General who is chief administrative officer of the UN and is appointed by the General Assembly, and an international staff.

Above: The symbol of the United Nations – a map of the world inside olive branches – signifies peace. It is shown here on the UN flag.

Left: The United Nations General Assembly has a huge auditorium where representatives from all the member countries can take part in the debates.

UNITED NATIONS MEMBER COUNTRIES

Country	Joined	Country	Joined	Country	Joined
Afghanistan	1946	Germany	1973	Papua New Guinea	1975
Albania	1955	Ghana	1957	Paraguay	1945
Algeria	1962	Greece	1945	Peru	1945
Angola	1976	Grenada	1974	Philippines	1945
Antigua and Barbuda	1981	Guatemala	1945	Poland	1945
Argentina	1945	Guinea	1958	Portugal	1955
Australia	1945	Guinea-Bissau	1974	Qatar	1971
Austria	1955	Guyana	1966	Romania	1955
Bahamas	1973	Haiti	1945	Rwanda	1962
Bahrain	1971	Honduras	1945	St Kitts–Nevis	1983
Bangladesh	1974	Hungary	1955	St Lucia	1979
Barbados	1966	Iceland	1946	St Vincent &	
Belgium	1945	India	1945	the Grenadines	1980
Belize	1981	Indonesia	1950	São Tomé & Principe	1975
Benin	1969	Iran	1945	Saudi Arabia	1945
Bhutan	1971	Iraq	1945	Senegal	1960
Bolivia	1945	Ireland, Rep. of	1955	Seychelles	1976
Botswana	1966	Israel	1949	Sierra Leone	1961
Brazil	1945	Italy	1955	Singapore	1965
Brunei	1984	Ivory Coast	1960	Solomon Islands	1978
Bulgaria	1955	Jamaica	1962	Somali Republic	1960
Burkina Faso	1960	Japan	1956	South Africa	1945
Burundi	1962	Jordan	1955	Spain	1955
Byelorussian SSR	1945	Kenya	1963	Sri Lanka	1955
Cambodia	1955	Kuwait	1963	Sudan	1956
Cameroon	1960	Laos	1955	Surinam	1975
Canada	1945	Lebanon	1945	Swaziland	1968
Cape Verde	1975	Lesotho	1966	Sweden	1946
Central African		Liberia	1945	Syria	1945
Republic	1960	Libya	1955	Tanzania	1961
Chad	1960	Luxembourg	1945	Thailand	1946
Chile	1945	Madagascar	1960	Togo	1960
China	1945	Malawi	1964	Trinidad & Tobago	1962
Colombia	1945	Malaysia	1957	Tunisia	1956
Comoros	1975	Maldives, Rep. of	1965	Turkey	1945
Congo	1960	Mali	1960	Uganda	1962
Costa Rica	1945	Malta	1964	Ukrainian SSR	1945
Cuba	1945	Mauritania	1961	USSR	1945
Cyprus	1960	Mauritius	1968	United Arab Emirates	1971
Czechoslovakia	1945	Mexico	1945	United Kingdom	1945
Denmark	1945	Mongolian PR	1961	United States	1945
Djibouti	1977	Morocco	1956	Uruguay	1945
Dominica	1978	Mozambique	1975	Vanuatu	1981
Dominican Republic	1945	Myanmar	1948	Venezuela	1945
Ecuador	1945	Nepal	1955	Vietnam	1976
Egypt	1945	Netherlands	1945	Western Samoa	1976
El Salvador	1945	New Zealand	1945	Yemen	1947
Equatorial Guinea	1968	Nicaragua	1945	Yugoslavia	1945
Ethiopia	1945	Niger	1960	Zaire	1960
Fiji	1970	Nigeria	1960	Zambia	1964
Finland	1955	Norway	1945	Zimbabwe	1980
France	1945	Oman	1971		
Gabon	1960	Pakistan	1947		
Gambia	1965	Panama	1945		

THE COMMONWEALTH OF NATIONS

This is a voluntary association of independent states. The Head of the Commonwealth is HM Queen Elizabeth II. Present members of the Commonwealth (with date of independence from British rule in brackets) are:

Antigua & Barbuda (1981), Australia (1901), Bahamas (1973), Bangladesh (from Pakistan, 1971), Barbados (1966), Belize (1981), Botswana (1966), Brunei (1984), Canada (1931), Cyprus (1960), Dominica (1978), *Fiji (1970), The Gambia (1965), Ghana (1957), Great Britain, Grenada (1974), Guyana (1966), India (1947), Jamaica (1962), Kenya (1963), Kiribati (1979), Lesotho (1966), Malawi (1964), Malaysia (1957), Maldives (1965), Malta (1964), Mauritius (1968), Nauru (1968), New Zealand (1907), Nigeria (1960), **Pakistan (1947), Papua New Guinea (1975), St Kitts-Nevis (1983), St Lucia (1979), St Vincent (1979), Seychelles (1976), Sierra Leone (1961), Singapore (1965), Solomon Islands (1978), Sri Lanka (1948), Swaziland (1968), Tanzania (1961), Tonga (1970), Trinidad & Tobago (1962), Tuvalu (1978), Uganda (1962), Vanuatu (1980), Western Samoa (1962), Zambia (1964), Zimbabwe (1980).

*Fiji's membership was suspended after the overthrow of the government in 1987 and the declaration of a republic.
** Pakistan left the Commonwealth in 1972, but rejoined in 1989.

Above: Jefferson, author of the Declaration of Independence.

Above: Eisenhower, leader of the Allied Forces in World War II.

AMERICAN PRESIDENTS

President (party)	Term	President (party)	Term
1 George Washington (F)	1789–97	23 Benjamin Harrison (R)	1889–93
2 John Adams (F)	1797–1801	24 Grover Cleveland (D)	1893–97
3 Thomas Jefferson (DR)	1801–09	25 William McKinley† (R)	1897–1901
4 James Madison (DR)	1809–17	26 Theodore Roosevelt (R)	1901–09
5 James Monroe (DR)	1817–25	27 William H. Taft (R)	1909–13
6 John Quincy Adams (DR)	1825–29	28 Woodrow Wilson (D)	1913–21
7 Andrew Jackson (D)	1829–37	29 Warren G. Harding* (R)	1921–23
8 Martin Van Buren (D)	1837–41	30 Calvin Coolidge (R)	1923–29
9 William H. Harrison* (W)	1841	31 Herbert C. Hoover (R)	1929–33
10 John Tyler (W)	1841–45	32 Franklin D. Roosevelt* (D)	1933–45
11 James K. Polk (D)	1845–49	33 Harry S. Truman (D)	1945–53
12 Zachary Taylor* (W)	1849–50	34 Dwight D. Eisenhower (R)	1953–61
13 Millard Fillmore (W)	1850–53	35 John F. Kennedy† (D)	1961–63
14 Franklin Pierce (D)	1853–57	36 Lyndon B. Johnson (D)	1963–69
15 James Buchanan (D)	1857–61	37 Richard M. Nixon (R)	1969–74
16 Abraham Lincoln† (R)	1861–65	38 Gerald R. Ford (R)	1974–77
17 Andrew Johnson (U)	1865–69	39 James E. Carter (D)	1977–80
18 Ulysses S. Grant (R)	1869–77	40 Ronald Reagan (R)	1980–89
19 Rutherford B. Hayes (R)	1877–81	41 George Bush (R)	1989–
20 James A. Garfield† (R)	1881		
21 Chester A. Arthur (R)	1881–85		
22 Grover Cleveland (D)	1885–89		

*Died in office   †Assassinated in office
F = Federalist. DR = Democratic–Republican.
D = Democratic. W = Whig. R = Republican. U = Union.

RULERS OF ENGLAND

Saxons

Egbert	827–839	Henry I	1100–1135
Ethelwulf	839–858	Stephen	1135–1154
Ethelbald	858–860	**House of Plantagenet**	
Ethelbert	860–866	Henry II	1154–1189
Ethelred I	866–871	Richard I	1189–1199
Alfred the Great	871–899	John	1199–1216
Edward the Elder	899–924	Henry III	1216–1272
Athelstan	924–939	Edward I	1272–1307
Edmund	939–946	Edward II	1307–1327
Edred	946–955	Edward III	1327–1377
Edwy	955–959	Richard II	1377–1399
Edgar	959–975	**House of Lancaster**	
Edward the Martyr	975–978	Henry IV	1399–1413
Ethelred I the Unready	978–1016	Henry V	1413–1422
Edmund Ironside	1016	Henry VI	1422–1461
Danes		**House of York**	
Canute	1016–1035	Edward IV	1461–1483
Harold I Harefoot	1035–1040	Edward V	1483
Hardicanute	1040–1042	Richard III	1483–1485
Saxons		**House of Tudor**	
Edward the Confessor	1042–1066	Henry VII	1485–1509
Harold II	1066	Henry VIII	1509–1547
House of Normandy		Edward VI	1547–1553
William I the Conqueror	1066–1087	Mary I	1553–1558
William II	1087–1100	Elizabeth I	1558–1603

RULERS OF SCOTLAND

Malcolm II	1005–1034	(*Interregnum* 1290–1292)	
Duncan I	1034–1040	John Balliol	1292–1296
Macbeth (usurper)	1040–1057	(*Interregnum* 1296–1306)	
Malcolm III Canmore	1057–1093	Robert I (Bruce)	1306–1329
Donald Bane	1093–1094	David II	1329–1371
Duncan II	1094	**House of Stuart**	
Donald Bane (restored)	1094–1097	Robert II	1371–1390
Edgar	1097–1107	Robert III	1390–1406
Alexander I	1107–1124	James I	1406–1437
David I	1124–1153	James II	1437–1460
Malcolm IV	1153–1165	James III	1460–1488
William the Lion	1165–1214	James IV	1488–1513
Alexander II	1214–1249	James V	1513–1542
Alexander III	1249–1286	Mary	1542–1567
Margaret of Norway	1286–1290	James VI (I of Great Britain)	1567–1625

RULERS OF BRITAIN

House of Stuart

James I	1603–1625	George III	1760–1820
Charles I	1625–1649	George IV	1820–1830
(*Commonwealth* 1649–1659)		William IV	1830–1837
Charles II	1660–1685	Victoria	1837–1901
James II	1685–1688	**House of Saxe-Coburg**	
William III } jointly	1689–1702	Edward VII	1901–1910
Mary II } jointly	1689–1694	**House of Windsor**	
Anne	1702–1714	George V	1910–1936
House of Hanover		Edward VIII	1936
George I	1714–1727	George VI	1936–1952
George II	1727-1760	Elizabeth II	1952–

BRITISH PRIME MINISTERS

Sir Robert Walpole (W)	1721–1742	Benjamin Disraeli (C)	1874–1880
Earl of Wilmington (W)	1742–1743	William Gladstone (L)	1880–1885
Henry Pelham (W)	1743–1754	Marquess of Salisbury (C)	1885–1886
Duke of Newcastle (W)	1754–1756	William Gladstone (L)	1886
Duke of Devonshire (W)	1756–1757	Marquess of Salisbury (C)	1886–1892
Duke of Newcastle (W)	1757–1762	William Gladstone (L)	1892–1894
Earl of Bute (T)	1762–1763	Earl of Rosebery (L)	1894–1895
George Grenville (W)	1763–1765	Marquess of Salisbury (C)	1895–1902
Marquess of Rockingham (W)	1765–1766	Arthur Balfour (C)	1902–1905
Earl of Chatham (W)	1766–1767	Sir Henry Campbell-	
Duke of Grafton (W)	1767–1770	Bannerman (L)	1905–1908
Lord North (T)	1770–1782	Herbert Asquith (L)	1908–1915
Marquess of Rockingham (W)	1782	Herbert Asquith (Cln)	1915–1916
Earl of Shelbourne (W)	1782–1783	David Lloyd-George (Cln)	1916–1922
Duke of Portland (Cln)	1783	Andrew Bonar Law (C)	1922–1923
William Pitt (T)	1783–1801	Stanley Baldwin (C)	1923–1924
Henry Addington (T)	1801–1804	James Ramsay	
William Pitt (T)	1804–1806	MacDonald (Lab)	1924
Lord Grenville (W)	1806–1807	Stanley Baldwin (C)	1924–1929
Duke of Portland (T)	1807–1809	James Ramsay	
Spencer Perceval (T)	1809–1812	MacDonald (Lab)	1929–1931
Earl of Liverpool (T)	1812–1827	James Ramsay	
George Canning (T)	1827	MacDonald (Cln)	1931–1935
Viscount Goderich (T)	1827–1828	Stanley Baldwin (Cln)	1935–1937
Duke of Wellington (T)	1828–1830	Neville Chamberlain (Cln)	1937–1940
Earl Grey (W)	1830–1834	Winston Churchill (Cln)	1940–1945
Viscount Melbourne (W)	1834	Winston Churchill (C)	1945
Sir Robert Peel (T)	1834–1835	Clement Attlee (Lab)	1945–1951
Viscount Melbourne (W)	1835–1841	Sir Winston Churchill (C)	1951–1955
Sir Robert Peel (T)	1841–1846	Sir Anthony Eden (C)	1955–1957
Lord John Russell (W)	1846–1852	Harold Macmillan (C)	1957–1963
Earl of Derby (T)	1852	Sir Alec Douglas-Home (C)	1963–1964
Earl of Aberdeen (P)	1852–1855	Harold Wilson (Lab)	1964–1970
Viscount Palmerston (L)	1855–1858	Edward Heath (C)	1970–1974
Earl of Derby (C)	1858–1859	Harold Wilson (Lab)	1974–1976
Viscount Palmerston (L)	1859–1865	James Callaghan (Lab)	1976–1979
Earl Russell (L)	1865–1866	Margaret Thatcher (C)	1979–1990
Earl of Derby (C)	1866–1868	John Major (C)	1990–
Benjamin Disraeli (C)	1868		
William Gladstone (L)	1868–1874		

W=Whig. T=Tory. Cln=Coalition. P=Peelite.
L=Liberal. C=Conservative. Lab=Labour.

TSARS OF RUSSIA

Ivan III the Great	1462–1505	Catherine I	1725–1727
Basil III	1505–1533	Peter II	1727–1730
Ivan IV the Terrible	1533–1584	Anna	1730–1740
Fëdor I	1584–1598	Ivan VI	1740–1741
Boris Godunov	1598–1605	Elizabeth	1741–1762
Fëdor II	1605	Peter III	1762
Demetrius	1605–1606	Catherine II the Great	1762–1796
Basil (IV) Shuiski	1606–1610	Paul I	1796–1801
[Interregnum, 1610–1613]		Alexander I	1801–1825
Michael Romanov	1613–1645	Nicholas I	1825–1855
Alexis	1645–1676	Alexander II	1855–1881
Fëdor III	1676–1682	Alexander III	1881–1894
Ivan V and Peter the Great	1682–1689	Nicholas II	1894–1917
Peter the Great	1689–1725		

ANIMAL SPEED RECORDS

	km/h	mph		km/h	mph		km/h	mph
Spine-tailed			Hare	72	45	Elephant	40	25
swift	170	106	Zebra	64	40	Sealion	40	25
Sailfish	109	68	Racehorse	64	40	Human	32	20
Cheetah	105	65	Shark	64	40	Black mamba	32	20
Pronghorn			Greyhound	63	39	Bee	18	11
antelope	97	60	Rabbit	56	35	Pig	18	11
Racing pigeon	97	60	Giraffe	51	32	Chicken	14	9
Lion	80	50	Grizzly bear	48	30	Spider	1·88	1·17
Gazelle	80	50	Cat	48	30	Tortoise	0·8	0·5
						Snail	0·05	0·03

TRADITIONAL ANNIVERSARY NAMES

It is sometimes the custom to give married couples gifts on their wedding anniversary that correspond to the traditional anniversary name.

Year	Name
1	paper
2	cotton
3	leather
4	fruit, flowers
5	wood
6	iron, sugar
7	wool, copper
8	bronze
9	pottery
10	tin, aluminium
11	steel
12	silk, fine linen
13	lace
14	ivory
15	crystal
20	china
25	silver
30	pearl
35	coral
40	ruby
45	sapphire
50	golden
55	emerald
60	diamond
75	platinum

SI UNITS

Basic units	Symbol	Measurement
metre	m	length
kilogram	kg	mass
second	s	time
ampere	A	electric current
kelvin	K	thermodynamic temperature
mole	mol	amount of substance
candela	cd	luminous intensity

Derived units*		
hertz	Hz	frequency
newton	N	force
pascal	Pa	pressure, stress
joule	J	energy, work, quantity of heat
watt	W	power, radiant flux
coulomb	C	electric charge, quantity of electricity
volt	V	electric potential, potential difference, emf
farad	F	capacitance
ohm	Ω	electric resistance
siemens	S	conductance
weber	Wb	magnetic flux
tesla	T	magnetic flux density
henry	H	inductance
lumen	lm	luminous flux
lux	lx	illuminance

Supplementary units		
radian	rad	plane angle
steradian	sr	solid angle

*These have special names; there are other derived units such as m^2 (area), mol/m^3 (concentration), m^3/l_2 (specific volume), etc.

PRINCIPAL LANGUAGES OF THE WORLD

Language	Speakers (millions)	Where spoken
Mandarin	575	China (north and east central)
English	360	UK and Commonwealth, Ireland, South Africa, USA
Hindi	170	India (north central)
Great Russian	170	USSR
Spanish	140	Spain, Central and South America (not Brazil)
German	100	Germany, Austria, Switzerland
Japanese	100	Japan
Bengali	90	Bangladesh, India (east)
Arabic	80	Middle East, North Africa
French	80	France and French Community, Canada
Malay/Indonesian*	80	Malaysia, Indonesia
Portuguese	80	Portugal, Brazil
Urdu	80	Pakistan
Italian	60	Italy
Cantonese	50	China (south)
Min	50	China (south and east)
Wu	50	China (east)
Javanese	45	Java
Telugu	45	India (south-east)
Ukrainian	41	USSR
Bihar	40	India (north-east)
Marathi	40	India (west)
Tamil	40	India (south-east), Sri Lanka
Korean	37	Korea
Punjabi	35	India (north)
Polish	33	Poland
Turkish	28	Turkey

*Officially called *Bahasa Indonesia* in Indonesia.

EARTH EXTREMES

Hottest shade temperature recorded: 57·7°C (136·4°F) at Al 'Aziziyah, Libya, on 13.9.22

Coldest temperature recorded: −88·3°C (−126·9°F) at Vostok, Antarctica, on 24.8.60

Highest annual average rainfall: 11,680 mm (460 in) at Mt Waialeale, Hawaii

Most rain in one month: 9300 mm (366.14 in) at Cherrapunji, India, in July 1861

Driest place on earth: Arica, Chile, averages 0·76 mm (0·03 in) of rain per year

Most snow in one year: 31,102 mm (1224·5 in) on Mt Rainier, Washington State, USA, 1971–2

Greatest ocean depth: 11,033 m (36,198 ft) Mariana Trench, Pacific Ocean

Greatest tides: 16·3 m (53·5 ft) Bay of Fundy, Nova Scotia, Canada

Strongest surface wind recorded: 372 km/h (231 mph) at Mt Washington, N.H., USA, in 1934

Deepest gorge: 2400 m (7874 ft) Hells Canyon, Idaho, USA

Longest gorge: 349 km (217 mi) Grand Canyon, Arizona, USA

Highest navigated lake: Titicaca, Peru/Bolivia, 3810 m (12,500 ft) above sea level

Deepest lake: Baikal, Siberia, USSR, 1940 m (6365 ft)

DAYS AND MONTHS

Day/Month	Named after
Sunday	the Sun
Monday	the Moon
Tuesday	Tiu, Norse god of war
Wednesday	Woden, Anglo-Saxon chief of gods
Thursday	Thor, Norse god of thunder
Friday	Frigg, Norse goddess
Saturday	Saturn, Roman god of harvests
January	Janus, Roman god of doors and gates
February	Februa, Roman period of purification
March	Mars, Roman god of war
April	aperire, Latin 'to open'
May	Maia, Roman goddess of spring and grow
June	Juno, Roman goddess of marriage
July	Julius Caesar
August	Augustus, first emperor of Rome
September	septem, Latin 'seven'
October	octo, Latin 'eight'
November	novem, Latin 'nine'
December	decem, latin 'ten'

BIRTHSTONES

Month	Hebrew	Present day
January	garnet	garnet
February	amethyst	amethyst
March	jasper	acquamarine bloodstone
April	sapphire	diamond
May	chalcedony carnelian agate	emerald chrysoprase
June	emerald	pearl moonstone alexandrite
July	onyx	ruby carnelian
August	carnelian	peridot sardonyx
September	chrysolite	sapphire lapis lazuli
October	aquamarine beryl	opal tourmaline
November	topaz	topaz
December	ruby	turquoise zircon

Above: Mackenzie discovered the largest river system in Canada.

Above: Pizzaro conquered the Inca empire in Peru.

Above: Balboa first sighted the Pacific Ocean in 1513.

EXPLORATION AND DISCOVERY

Place	Achievement	Explorer or discoverer	Date
World	circumnavigated	Ferdinand Magellan (Port. for Sp.)	1519–21
Pacific Ocean	discovered	Vasco Núñez de Balboa (Sp.)	1513
Africa			
River Congo (mouth)	discovered	Diogo Cão (Port.)	c. 1483
Cape of Good Hope	sailed round	Bartolomeu Diaz (Port.)	1488
River Niger	explored	Mungo Park (GB)	1795
River Zambezi	discovered	David Livingstone (GB)	1851
Sudan	explored	Heinrich Barth (Germ. for GB)	1852–5
Victoria Falls	discovered	Livingstone	1855
Lake Tanganyika	discovered	Richard Burton & John Speke (GB)	1858
River Congo	traced	Sir Henry Stanley (GB)	1877
Asia			
China	visited	Marco Polo (Ital.)	c. 1272
India (Cape route)	visited	Vasco da Gama (Port.)	1498
Japan	visited	St Francis-Xavier (Sp.)	1549
China	explored	Ferdinand Richthofen (Germ.)	1868
North America			
North America	discovered	Leif Ericsson (Norse)	c. 1000
West Indies	discovered	Christopher Columbus (Ital. for Sp.)	1492
Newfoundland	discovered	John Cabot (Ital. for Eng.)	1497
Mexico	conquered	Hernando Cortés (Sp.)	1519–21
St Lawrence River	explored	Jacques Cartier (Fr.)	1534–6
Mississippi River	discovered	Hernando de Soto (Sp.)	1541
Canadian interior	explored	Samuel de Champlain (Fr.)	1603–9
Hudson Bay	discovered	Henry Hudson (Eng.)	1610
Alaska	discovered	Vitus Bering (Dan. for Russ.)	1728
South America			
South America	visited	Columbus	1498
Venezuela	explored	Alonso de Ojeda (Sp.)	1499
Brazil	discovered	Pedro Alvares Cabral (Port.)	1500
Tierra del Fuego	discovered	Magellan	1520
Peru	explored	Francisco Pizarro (Sp.)	1530–8
River Amazon	explored	Francisco de Orellana (Sp.)	1541
Cape Horn	discovered	Willem Schouten (Dut.)	1616
Australasia, Polar regions, etc			
Greenland	visited	Eric the Red (Norse)	c. 982
Spitsbergen	discovered	Willem Barents (Dut.)	1596
Australia	visited	Abel Tasman (Dut.)	1642
New Zealand	sighted	Tasman	1642
New Zealand	visited	James Cook (GB)	1769
Antarctica	sighted	Nathaniel Palmer (US)	1820
Antarctica	circumnavigated	Fabian von Bellingshausen (Russ.)	1819–21
Australian interior	explored	Charles Sturt (GB)	1828
Antarctica	explored	Charles Wilkes (US)	1838–42
Australia	crossed (S–N)	Robert Burke (Ir.) & William Wills (GB)	1860–1
Greenland	explored	Fridtjof Nansen (Nor.)	1888
North Pole	reached	Robert Peary (US)	1909
South Pole	reached	Roald Amundsen (Nor.)	1911
Antarctica	crossed	Sir Vivian Fuchs (GB)	1957–8

GEOLOGICAL TIME SCALE

Eras	Periods	Epochs	Millions of years ago	Lifeforms
CENOZOIC	Quaternary	Holocene (recent)	0·01	(End of ice age)
		Pleistocene		(Ice ages) Mammoths, woolly rhinoceroses. Development of modern human beings
	Tertiary	Pliocene	2 / 7	Mammals spread; earliest human creatures
		Miocene		Whales and apes
		Oligocene	26	Modern types of mammals
		Eocene	38	First horses and elephants
		Palaeocene	54	Early mammals
MESOZOIC	Cretaceous		64	End of dinosaurs; flowering plants spread
	Jurassic		136	Giant dinosaurs; first birds
	Triassic		195	Small dinosaurs; first mammals
PALAEOZOIC	Permian			Rapid increase in reptiles
	Carboniferous (Pennsylvanian and Mississippian)		280	Forests formed coal; first reptiles; first insects
	Devonian		345	First forests and land animals, amphibians. Age of fishes.
	Silurian		410	First land plants. First jawed fishes
	Ordovician		440	First vertebrates – armoured fish – appear in the sea
	Cambrian		530	Fossils abundant in rocks. All major groups of invertebrates represented
PRE-CAMBRIAN	Proterozoic		570	Sea animals without backbones; seaweeds
	Archaeozoic		1,850	First primitive plants and animals
	Azoic		4,000 about 4,500	(Earliest known rocks) (Earth formed)

GREAT COMPOSERS

Bach, Johann Sebastian (1685–1750) German composer born at Eisenach; the most distinguished in a long line of musicians. Bach's vast output can be divided into three groups: organ works; instrumental and orchestral works; and religious choral works.

△ German composer, Johann Sebastian Bach (1685–1750).

Beethoven, Ludgwig van (1770–1827) German composer, one of the outstanding figures of Western music. His symphonies, overtures, concertos, piano sonatas and string quartets are considered some of the world's greatest.

Brahms, Johannes (1833–97) German composer. His works include four symphonies, two piano concertos, a violin concerto and a double concerto (violin and cello), chamber music, piano music and many songs and choral compositions.

Britten Benjamin (1913–76) One of the outstanding 20th century British composers, and a brilliant pianist, Britten was especially noted for his operas, choral music and songs.

Chopin, Fryderyk, or **Frédéric** (1810–49) Polish piano virtuoso and composer, known almost entirely for piano music.

Dvořák, Antonín (1841–1904) Czech composer. From 1892–5 was in the United States as Director of the National Conservatory in New York, where he wrote his best-known work, the symphony *From the New World*.

Gershwin, George (1898–1937) American composer and pianist whose combination of American styles (jazz and blues) with impressionist harmony was a major influence on 20th century American music.

Handel, George Frideric (1685–1759) German-born composer of Italian operas and, later, oratorios (music dramas) mainly on religious themes; *Messiah* is the most famous.

Handel also wrote many instrumental compositions.

Haydn, Franz Joseph (1732–1809) Prolific Austrian composer whose development of the sonata-symphony form and style earned him the title of 'Father of the Symphony'.

Mahler, Gustav (1860–1911) Bohemian-born composer noted for his symphonies, written in late German-romantic style.

Mozart, Wolfgang Amadeus (1756–1791) Austrian composer, born in Salzburg. As a child prodigy, he toured Europe giving piano recitals with his sister and father. For speed and ease of composition Mozart was unrivalled, producing in his short life over 600 works.

Schubert, Franz Peter (1797–1828) Austrian composer. In a career even shorter than Mozart's. Schubert achieved a large output ranging from symphonies and operas to chamber music and over 500 songs.

Stravinsky, Igor (1882–1971) Russian-born composer and one of the key figures of 20th century music. Made his reputation with a series of remarkable ballets, including *The Firebird*, *Petrushka* and *The Rite of Spring*.

Tchaikovsky, Peter Ilyich (1840–93) Russian composer, the first to become widely popular outside his country. His work was notable for its melodic flair, emotional content and vivid orchestration.

◁ Beethoven's early music was influenced by Mozart and Haydn.

SOME OPERATIC TERMS

aria (Italian, 'air') A solo.

ballad opera Simple kind of opera, made up of popular tunes interspersed with spoken dialogue.

comic opera Opera with a farcical plot.

finale Closing portion of act or opera; usually whole company sings together.

folk opera Opera based on folk music and folk tales.

grand opera Opera with libretto entirely set to music.

intermezzo Instrumental piece interposed between scenes or acts of opera, also called interlude.

SOME BALLET TERMS

arabesque Position in which dancer stands on one leg with arms extended, body bent forward from hips, while other leg is stretched out backwards.

attitude Position in which dancer stretches one leg backwards, bending it a little at the knee so that lower part of leg is parallel to floor.

ballerina Female ballet dancer.

barre Exercise bar fixed to classroom wall at hip level; dancers grasp it when exercising.

battement Beating movement made by raising and lowering leg, sideways, backwards or forwards.

entrechat Leap in which dancer rapidly crosses and uncrosses feet in air.

fouetté Turn in which dancer whips free leg round.

glissade Gliding movement.

jeté Leap from one foot to another.

pas Any dance step.

pas de deux Dance for two.

pas seule Solo dance.

pirouette Movement in which dancer spins completely round on one foot.

choreography Art of dance composition.

corps de ballet Main body of ballet dancers, as distinct from soloists.

TIME

Second (s, or sec)
60 s = 1 minute (min)
60 min = 1 hour (h or hr)
24 hr = 1 day (d)
7 days = 1 week
365¼ days = 1 year
10 years = 1 decade
100 years = 1 century
1,000 years = 1 millennium
1 mean solar day =24 h 3 min 56.555 s
1 sidereal day = 23 h 56 min 4.091 s
1 solar, tropical, or equinoctial year = 365.2422 d (365 d 5 h 48 min 46 s)
1 sidereal year = 365.2564 d (365 d 6 h 9 min 9.5 s)
1 synodic (lunar) month = 27.3217 d
1 lunar year = 354.3672 d = 12 synodic months

CAPACITY

Metric units
millilitre (ml)
1,000 ml = 1 litre (l)
100 l = 1 hectolitre (hl)

Imperial units
gill
4 gills = 1 pint
2 pints = 1 quart
4 quarts = 1 gallon = 277.274 cu in

Dry
2 gallons = 1 peck
4 pecks = 1 bushel
8 bushels = 1 quarter
36 bushels = 1 chaldron

Apothecaries' fluid
minim (min)
60 min = 1 fluid drachm (fl dr)
8 fl dr = 1 fluid ounce (fl oz)
5 fl oz = 1 gill
20 fl oz = 1 pint

WEIGHT

Metric units
milligram (mg)
1,000 mg = 1 gram (g)
1,000 g = 1 kilogram (kg)
100 kg = 1 quintal (q)
1,000 kg = 1 metric ton, or tonne (t)

Imperial units (Avoirdupois)
grain (gr); dram (dr)
7,000 gr = 1 pound (lb)
16 dr = 1 ounce (oz)
16 oz = 1 lb
14 lb = 1 stone
28 lb = 1 quarter
112 lb = 1 hundredweight (cwt)
20 cwt = 1 ton = 2240 lb

Troy weight
24 gr = 1 pennyweight (dwt)
20 dwt = 1 (Troy) ounce = 480 gr

Apothecaries' weight
20 gr = 1 scruple
3 scruples = 1 drachm
8 drachms = 1 (apoth) ounce = 480 gr

CONVERSION FACTORS

If measurements are in imperial, multiply by the conversion factors given below to find the metric equivalent; if they are in metric, divide by the conversion factors to find imperial.

1 acre = 0.4047 hectares
1 bushel (imp.) = 36.369 litres
1 centimetre = 0.3937 inch
1 chain = 20.1168 metres
1 cord = 3.62456 cubic metres
1 cubic centimetre = 0.0610 cubic inch
1 cubic decimetre = 61.024 cubic inches
1 cubic foot = 0.0283 cubic metre
1 cubic inch = 16.387 cubic centimetres
1 cubic metre = 35.3146 cubic feet = 1.3079 cubic yards
1 cubic yard = 0.7646 cubic metre
1 fathom = 1.8288 metres
1 fluid oz (apoth.) = 28.4131 millilitres
1 fluid oz = 28.4 millilitres
1 foot = 0.3048 metre = 30.48 centimetres
1 foot per second = 0.6818 mph = 1.097 km/h
1 gallon (imperial) = 4.5461 litres
1 gallon (US liquid) = 3.7854 litres
1 gill = 0.142 litre
1 gram = 0.0353 ounce = 0.002205 pound = 15.43 grains = 0.0321 ounce (Troy)
1 hectare = 2.4710 acres
1 hundredweight = 50.80 kilograms

1 inch = 2.54 centimetres
1 kilogram = 2.2046 pounds
1 kilometre = 0.6214 mile = 1093.6 yards
1 knot (international) = 0.5144 metres /sec = 1.852 km/h
1 litre = 0.220 gallon (imperial) = 0.2642 gallon (US) = 1.7598 pints (imperial) = 0.8799 quarts
1 metre = 39.3701 in = 3.2808 ft = 1.0936 yd
1 metric tonne = 0.9842 ton
1 mile (statute) = 1.6093 kilometres
1 mile (nautical) = 1.852 kilometres
1 millimetre = 0.03937 inch
1 ounce = 28.350 grams
1 peck (imperial) = 9.0922 litres
1 pennyweight = 1.555 grams
1 pica (printer's) = 4.2175 millimetres
1 pint (imperial) – 0.5683 litre
1 pound = 0.4536 kilogram
1 quart (imperial) = 1.1365 litres
1 square centimetre = 0.1550 square inch
1 square foot = 0.0929 square metre
1 square inch = 6.4516 square centimetres
1 square kilometre = 0.3860 square mile
1 square metre = 10.7639 square feet = 1.1960 square yards
1 square mile = 2.5900 square kilometres
1 square yard = 0.8361 square metre
1 ton = 1.0160 square metre
1 yard = 0.9144 metre

HISTORICAL UNITS

Where used	Current equivalent
Cubit (elbow to finger tip)	
Egypt (2650 BC)	52.4 cm (20.6 in)
Babylon (1500 BC)	53.0 cm (20.9 in)
Hebrew	45 cm (17.7 in)
Black Cubit (Arabia AD 800s)	54.1 cm (21.3 in)
Mexico (Aztec)	52.5 cm (20.7 in)
Ancient China	53.2 cm (20.9 in)
Ancient Greece	46.3 cm (18.2 in)
Ancient Rome	44.4 cm (17.4 in)
England	45.7 cm (18.0 in)
Northern Cubit (c.3000 BC–AD 1800s)	67.6 cm (26.6 in)

Where used	Current equivalent
Foot (length of foot)	
Athens	31.6 cm (12.44 in)
Rome	29.6 cm (11.66 in)
Northern	33.5 cm (13.19 in)
England (Medieval)	33.5 cm (13.19 in)
France	32.5 cm (12.79 in)

Ancient Roman units

1 digitus	1.85 cm (0.73 in)
4 digiti = 1 palmus	7.4 cm (2.9 in)
4 palmi =1 pes	29.6 cm (11.7 in)
5 pes = 1 passus	1.48 m (4.86 ft)
125 passus = 1 stadium	185 m (202.3 yd)

THE WORLD'S HOT AND COLD REGIONS

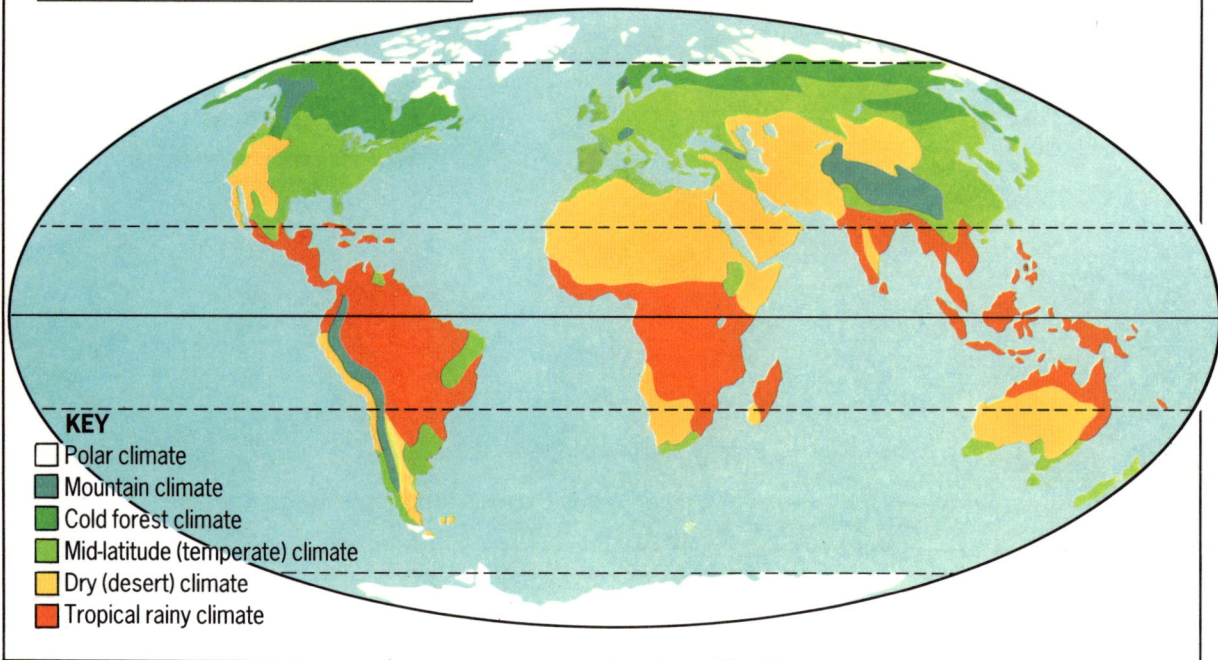

KEY
- Polar climate
- Mountain climate
- Cold forest climate
- Mid-latitude (temperate) climate
- Dry (desert) climate
- Tropical rainy climate

SOME WEATHER TERMS

climate The average weather conditions of a place. Climate figures are averages of figures collected over a number of years, so extremes of heat and cold, drought and flood are hidden.

hurricane A severe tropical storm with spiralling winds and very low air pressure. The wind does a great deal of damage, the accompanying rain and high tides cause floods.

Mediterranean climate Summers are hot and dry; winters are warm and wet. Such a climate is found around the Mediterranean Sea and also in central California and Perth, Western Australia.

monsoon The word means season and usually refers to winds that bring an exceptionally wet season for part of the year. The most spectacular monsoon climates are in Asia.

temperate lands Those parts of the world between the tropics and the Polar areas which have a cold season and a hot season. Places such as the Mediterranean which have warm winters may be called warm temperate.

precipitation When used of the weather, refers to rain and snow.

WEATHER EXTREMES

Hottest shade temperature recorded: 57.7°C (136°F) at Al'Aziziyah, Libya, on September 13, 1992.

Coldest temperature recorded: –89.2°C (–128.6°F) at Vostock, Antarctica, on July 21, 1983.

Highest average annual rainfall: 11,770 mm (463 inches) at Tutunendo, Colombia.

Driest place on earth: Arica, Chile, averages 0.76 mm (0.030 inches) of rain per year.

BEAUFORT SCALE

In 1805 Admiral Sir Francis Beaufort worked out a scale for measuring wind speed. The scale is numbered from 1 to 12 and represents wind force out in the open, 10 metres (33 feet) above the ground.

No.	Wind force	km/h	mph	Observable effects
0	calm	<1.6	<1	smoke rises vertically
1	light air	1.6–4.8	1–3	direction shown by smoke
2	slight breeze	6.4–11.3	4–7	felt on face; wind vanes move
3	gentle breeze	12.9–19.3	8–12	leaves, twigs move; flags extended
4	moderate breeze	20.9–29.0	13–18	dust, paper, small branches move
5	fresh breeze	30.6–38.6	19–24	small trees sway; flags ripple
6	strong breeze	40.2–50.0	25–31	large branches move; flags beat
7	moderate gale	51.5–61.2	32–38	whole trees sway; walking difficult
8	fresh gale	62.8–74.0	39–46	twigs break off; walking hindered
9	strong gale	–75.6–86.9	47–54	slight damage – chimney-pots, slates
10	whole gale	–88.5–101.4	55–63	severe damage; trees uprooted
11	storm	103.0–115.9	64–72	widespread damage
12	hurricane	>117.5	>73	devastation

EARTH'S VITAL STATISTICS

Age: about 4600 million years
Weight: about 6000 million million tonnes
Diameter: from Pole to Pole through the Earth's centre 12,719 km across the Equator through the Earth's centre 12,757 km
Circumference: round the Poles 40,020 km round the Equator 40,091 km
Area of water: about 361 million sq km – 71 per cent
Area of land: about 149 million sq km – 29 per cent
Volume: 1,084,000 million cubic km
Average height of land: 840 metres above sea level
Average depth of ocean: 3795 metres below sea level

MOON FACTS

The moon is 382,000 kilometres from the Earth.
The Earth weighs 81 times as much as the Moon.
The diameter (distance across) of the Moon is 3476 kilometres.
The oldest Moon rock is 4600 million years old.
The Moon has no seas. Its flat plains are called maria, because early astronomers mistook them for oceans and named them after the Latin *mare*, meaning 'sea'.
The Moon's surface is pitted with craters. Almost all these holes were made by meteorites crashing into the Moon.
The Latin word for the Moon is *luna*. From this we get our word 'lunar'.

HOW THE PLANETS FORMED

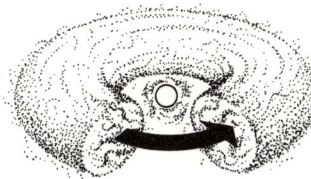

1. In the beginning, there was a spinning ring of gas and dust particles, circling the Sun.

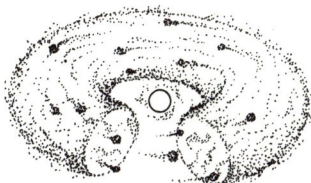

2. The solid particles began to stick together, forming larger bodies, made mostly of carbon and ice.

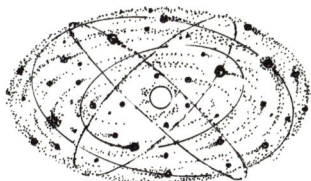

3. The bodies became as big as planets, and began to 'pull' against each other. Some of the very small ice bodies became comets.

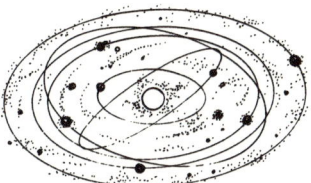

4. Eventually there were just nine large bodies going around the Sun in orbits: the major planets.

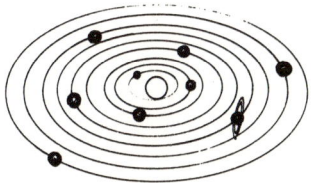

5. In time, the planets' orbits stabilized.

INSIDE THE EARTH

The Earth's **outer core** lies below the mantle and above the inner core. It is 2240 km thick. The outer core is made mainly of metals, under enormous pressure and so hot they are molten (melted). Four-fifths of it may be iron and nickel. The rest is probably silicon.

The **inner core** is a solid ball, about 2240 km across. Like the outer core, it may be made mainly of iron and nickel. The core temperature is 3700°C and the pressure there is 3800 tonnes per square centimetre.

The **mantle** lies beneath the crust and above the outer core. Nearly 2900 km thick, the mantle is made up of hot rocks. Temperature and pressure here are lower than in the core. Even so, much of the mantle rock is semi-molten.

The **crust** is the Earth's solid outer layer. It is up to 30 km thick beneath mountains, but only 6 km thick under the oceans. Its rocks float on the denser rocks of the mantle.

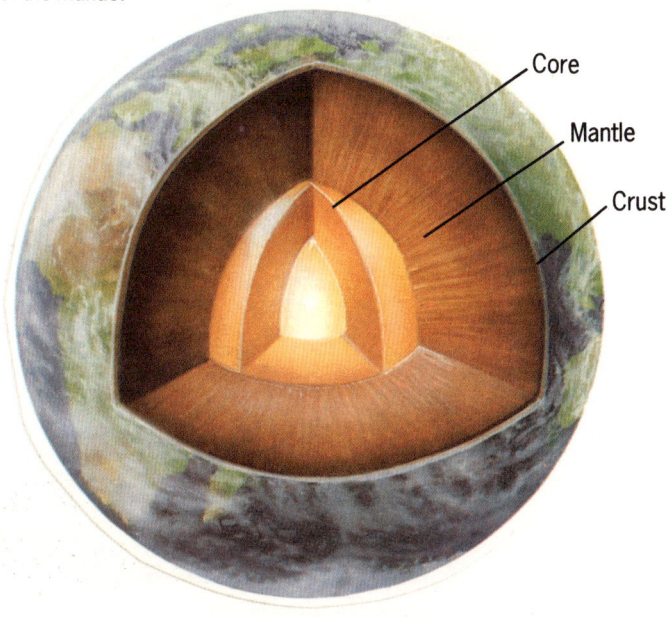

Core
Mantle
Crust

LONGEST RIVERS

	km	mi
Nile (Africa)	6670	4145
Amazon (S America)	6437	4000
Chang Jiang (China)	6380	3964
Mississippi–Missouri–Red Rock (N America)	6231	3872
Ob-Irtysh (USSR)	5150	3200
Huang He (China)	4672	2903
Zaire* (Africa)	4828	3000
Lena (USSR)	4828	3000
Amur (Asia)	4506	2800
Yenisey (USSR)	4506	2800
Mekong (SE Asia)	4184	2600
Niger (Africa)	4000	2486

*Formerly Congo River

LARGEST ISLANDS

	sq km	sq mi
Greenland (N Atlantic)	2,175,000	840,050
New Guinea (SW Pacific)	794,090	306,600
Borneo (SW Pacific)	751,078	289,993
Madagascar (Indian Ocean)	587,041	226,670
Baffin I. (Canadian Arctic)	476,066	183,810
Sumatra (Indian Ocean)	431,982	166,789
Great Britain (N Atlantic)	229,522	88,619
Honshu (NW Pacific)	226,087	87,293
Ellesmere (Canadian Arctic)	198,393	76,600
Victoria I. (Canadian Arctic)	192,695	74,400

LARGEST LAKES

	sq km	sq mi
Caspian Sea (USSR/Iran)	438,695	169,390
Superior (USA/Canada)	82,409	31,820
Victoria (Africa)	69,484	26,828
Aral (USSR)	67,770	26,166
Huron (USA/Canada)	59,570	23,000
Michigan (USA)	58,016	22,400
Tanganyika (Africa)	31,999	12,355
Great Bear (Canada)	31,598	12,200
Baikal (USSR)	31,499	12,162
Malawi* (Africa)	28,490	11,000

*Also called Lake Nyasa

MAJOR WATERFALLS

Highest	m	ft
Angel Falls (Venezuela)	979	3212
Yosemite Falls (California)	739	2425
Mardals Fossen (Norway)	655	2149
Greatest Volume	**m³/sec**	**ft³/sec**
Guaira (Brazil/Paraguay)	13,300	470,000
Niagara (N America)	6000	212,200

HIGHEST MOUNTAINS

Asia	m	ft
Everest (Himalaya–Nepal/Tibet)	8848	29,028
K2 Godwin Austen (Pakistan/India)	8611	28,250
Kanchenjunga (Himalaya–Nepal/Sikkim)	8579	28,146
Makalu (Himalaya–Nepal/Tibet)	8470	27,790
Dhaulagiri (Himalaya–Nepal)	8172	26,810
Nanga Parbat (Himalaya–India)	8126	26,660
Annapurna (Himalaya–Nepal)	8075	26,492
Gasherbrum (Karakoram–India)	8068	26,470
Gosainthan (Himalaya–Tibet)	8013	26,291
Nanda Devi (Himalaya–India)	7817	25,645
South America		
Aconcagua (Andes–Argentina)	6960	22,835
North America		
McKinley (Alaska–USA)	6194	20,322
Africa		
Kilimanjaro (volcanic–Tanzania)	5895	19,341
Europe		
Elbruz (Caucasus–USSR)	5633	18,481
Mont Blanc (Alps–France)	4810	15,781
Antarctica		
Vinson Massif	5139	16,860
Australasia		
Jaya (New Guinea)	5029	16,500

OCEANS

	sq km	sq mi
Pacific	181,000,000	70,000,000
Atlantic	106,000,000	41,000,000
Indian	73,490,000	28,375,000
Arctic	14,350,000	5,541,000

Above: Large waterfalls are awesome sights.

SEVEN WONDERS OF THE WORLD*
*Originally compiled by Antipater of Sidon, a Greek poet, in the 100s BC.

Pyramids of Egypt Oldest and only surviving 'wonder'. Built in the 2000s BC as royal tombs, about 80 are still standing. The largest, the Great Pyramid of Cheops, at el-Gizeh, was 147 metres (482 feet) high when new.

Hanging Gardens of Babylon Terraced gardens adjoining Nebuchadnezzar's palace said to rise from 23 to over 90 metres (75 to 295 feet). Supposedly built by the king about 600 BC to please his wife, a princess from the mountains, but they are also associated with the Assyrian Queen Semiramis.

Statue of Zeus at Olympia Carved by Phidias, the 12-metre (39-foot) statue marked the site of the original Olympic Games in the 400s BC. It was constructed of ivory and gold, and showed Zeus (Jupiter) on his throne.

Temple of Artemis (Diana) at Ephesus Constructed of Parian marble and more than 122 metres (400 feet) long with over 100 columns 18 metres (59 feet) high, it was begun about 350 BC and took some 120 years to build. Destroyed by the Goths in AD 262.

Mausoleum at Halicarnassus Erected by Queen Artemisia in memory of her husband King Mausolus of Caria (in Asia Minor), who died 353 BC. It stood 43 metres (141 feet) high. The only remains are a few pieces in the British Museum and the word 'mausoleum' in the English language.

Colossus of Rhodes Gigantic bronze statue of sun-god Helios (or Apollo); stood about 36 metres (118 feet) high, dominating the harbour entrance at Rhodes. The sculptor Chares supposedly laboured for 12 years before he completed it in 280 BC. It was destroyed by an earthquake in 244 BC.

Pharos of Alexandria Marble lighthouse and watchtower built about 270 BC on the island of Pharos in Alexandria's harbour. Possibly standing 122 metres (400 feet) high, it was destroyed by an earthquake in 1375.

Pyramids of Egypt

Colossus of Rhodes

Statue of Zeus

Mausoleum at Halicarnassus

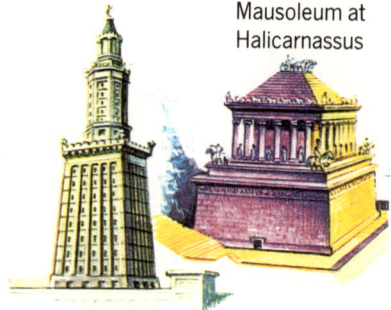

Pharos of Alexandria

Above: Some of the Seven Wonders of the World as they may have looked. Only the Egyptian pyramids have survived.

INDEX

Figures *in italics* indicate pictures or information in picture captions

A

Aborigines 50
Adelaide 50
advertising *26*
Afghanistan, statistics 65
Africa 19, 30–32, *30–32*, 34–35
  animals *34–35*
  colonies map 33
  colonization 35
  farming 34
  industries 34
  languages 32
  map *31*
  population 19, 35
  transport 34
agnostics 21
Alaska *38*
Albania, statistics 68
albatross *60*
Algeria 34
  statistics 62
Allah 20
Alps 52
Amazon, River 41
American football *23*
American Indians *38*
Andes Mountains 41
Andorra, statistics 68
Angola, statistics 62
Anguilla, statistics 71
animals
  speed records 82
anniversary names 82
Antarctic 60, *60*
  map of *61*
Antigua and Barbuda, statistics 71
apartheid 35
Arctic 60, *60*
  map of *61*
Arctic Ocean 60
Arctic tern 61
Argentina, statistics 73
Ascension Island, statistics 62
Asia 23, 42–43, *42–43*, 46–47
  farming 43
  industry 43
  map *44–45*
  population growth 19
  trade 26, 47
atheists 21
Atlantic Ocean 10–11
atmosphere 12
atoll *8*
Auckland 48
Australasia 48, 50–51
  map *49*

population growth 19
Australia 26, 48–51, 74
  climate 51
  deserts 50
  farming 51
  immigrants 50
  industry 51
  mining 51
  outback *49*
  statistics 74
  trade 26
Austria, statistics 68
Aztecs 39

B

badger *59*
Bahamas, statistics 71
Bahrain, statistics 65
Balboa, Vasco Nuñez de *84*
Bali school 47
Bangladesh 43
  population 46
  statistics 65
bar mitzvah *21*
Barbados, statistics 71
bartering *27*
batholiths 8
bathyscaphe 10
bats *59*
bauxite 34
Beaufort Scale (wind) 12
Belgium, statistics 68
beliefs 20–21, *20–21*
Belize, statistics 71
Benin, statistics 62
Berbers 31
Berlin Wall *52*
Bermuda, statistics 71
Bhutan, statistics 65
Birmingham 58
birthstones 83
Black Africans 31
Bolivia, statistics 73
Bora Bora *51*
Botswana, statistics 62
Brahman 20
Brahmaputra, River 42
Brazil 41, *41*
  statistics 73
Britain 11, 55
  prime ministers of 81
  rulers of 80
  statistics 70
  see also United Kingdom
Brunei, statistics 65
Buddha, the 21
Buddhism 46
buffalo *35*
Bulgaria, statistics 68
Burkina Faso, statistics 62
Burton, Sir Richard *30*
Burundi, statistics 62

C

Cambodia 47
  statistics 66
camel *34*
  caravans 47
Cameroon, statistics 62
Canada 26, 38
  farming 38
  industry 38
  statistics 71
  trade 26
Caribbean Sea 39
Caroline Islands 48
Caspian Sea 53
Caucasoids 18–19
Cayman Islands, statistics 71
Central African Republic, statistics 62
Central America 19, 36
  climate 39
  population growth 19
Chad *33*
  statistics 62
Chang Jiang (Yangzte River) 42
Charles I (England) *25*
Chartres Cathedral, France *21*
Chicago 38
Chile, statistics, 73
China 26–27, 42, 43, 66
  farming 43
  industry 27, 43
  population 42
  statistics 66
  trade 26, *26*
Christianity 20–21, 46
civil rights *24*
Civil War, English, 25, *25*
climate 12
cloud types *13*
cobalt 34
cobra 47
Cold War 56
Colombia, statistics 74
Columbus, Christopher 39
Common Market 56
Commonwealth of Nations 79
Comoros, statistics 62
conifers 15
Confucianism 21
Congo, statistics 62
continental drift 9
continental shelf *10*
convict settlement 50
Cook Islands, statistics 74
copper 34
coral reef 8
core (of Earth) 8

Costa Rice, statistics 71
cotton 26
court (law) *25*
cricket *23*
crocodiles *19*, 35
crust (of Earth) 8
  oceanic 10
Cuba 39
  statistics 71
Cyprus statistics 68
Czechoslovakia statistics 68

D

Danube, River 54
days and months 83
deciduous trees 15
democracy 24
Denmark, statistics 68
depression *13*
deserts *14*, 14–15, 30
developed countries 29
developing countries 29
diamond 32
Djibouti, statistics 62
Dominica, statistics 71
Dominican Republic statistics 71
donkey *34*
duck *59*
Dusseldorf 58
dyke 8

E

Earth 8–10, 18–19, 83, 85
  geological time scale 85
  inhabitable area 18
  magnetism 8
  plates 10
  records 83
  structure 8
earthquakes 8
Easter Island 48
Ecuador, statistics 74
Egypt 20, 26, 34–35, 62
  industry 34
  statistics 62
  trade 26
Egypt, Ancient religion 20, *20*
Eisenhower, Dwight David *82*
El Salvador 39
  statistics 71
England, rulers of 80
environment 14–17, *14–17*
Equator 12
Equatorial Guinea, statistics 63
Eskimo *61*

Ethiopia, statistics 63
Euphrates, River 42
Europe 19, *52–59*
  animals 59
  climate 52
  emigration 57
  empires 55
  farming 54
  finance 57
  fishing 58
  industry 57
  languages 55
  map *53*
  minerals 54
  national costumes 58
  plant life 52
  population growth 19
  trade 56
  transport 57
  travel 58
European Community 56
exercise 22
exploration and discovery, table 84

F

Falkland Islands statistics 74
famine 32
farming 32
fencing *23*
Fiji 48, 51
  statistics 74
Finland, statistics 68
flags 28
  Africa *33*
  Asia *45*
  Australasia *50*
  Europe *57*
  North America *36*
  South America *40*
fossils 35
fox *59*
France 55
  statistics 68
French Guiana, statistics 74
French Polynesia, statistics 74
Friesian cows 58

G

Gabon, statistics 63
Gambia, statistics 63
game reserves 30
Ganesh *20*
Ganges, River 42
gas 39
gauchos 41
geological periods 85
geology 8–10, *8–10*
Germany, statistics 69
Germany, West economic revival 26

Geronimo *38*
Ghana, statistics 63
giant panda *47*
Gibraltar, statistics 69
Gobi Desert 42
gold 32
Gondwanaland 9
government 24–25, *24–25*
Great Barrier Reef 50
Great Lakes 36
Great Rift Valley 30
Greater Antilles 39
Greece 20, 54
  democracy 24
  religion *20*
  statistics 69
Greenland, statistics 69
Grenada, statistics 72
Guadeloupe, statistics 72
Guam, statistics 75
Guatemala 39
  statistics 72
Guinea, statistics 63
Guinea Bissau, statistics 63
Gulf of Mexico 11
Guyana, statistics 74
gymnastics *22*

H
habitats 14
Hagia Sophia mosque *21*
Haiti, statistics *72*
Hawaii 48
hedgehog 59
hereditary rule 24
Himalayas 42
Hinduism 20, *20*, 46
Hispaniola 39
Homo sapiens 72
Honduras, statistics 72
Hong Kong *47*, 66
Huang He, River 42
humans 35
Hungary, statistics 69
hurricane *12*

I
Iceland, statistics 69
India 26–27, *43*, 46
  farming 43, *46*
  industry 27, 43
  population 46
  statistics 66
  trade 250
Indonesia 47, *47*
  statistics 66
Indus, River 42
Industrial Revolution 26–27, 56
Iran, statistics 66
Iraq, statistics 66
Ireland, Republic of, statistics 69
Irrawaddy, River 42
Islam 20, *21*, 46
islands, table of 90
Israel 43
  statistics 66
Italy, statistics 69
Ivory Coast, statistics 63

J
Jaipur, temple *43*
Jamaica 39
  statistics *72*
Japan
  economic revival 26
  industry 43, 46
  population 46
  statistics 66
  temple *43*
Jefferson, Thomas *82*
Jesus Christ 20–21
Jews
  religion 20, *20*
Jordan, statistics 66
Judaism 20, *21*

K
kangaroo *51*
Kenya, statistics 63
Kenya, Mount 30
Kilimanjaro, Mount 30, 90
Kiribati 48
  statistics 73
kiwi *51*
koala bear 51
kookaburra *51*
Koran 20
Korea, North 47
  statistics 66
Korea, South 27
  statistics 66
kudu *35*
Kuwait 43
  statistics 66

L
lakes, table of 90
languages 18
  table of 83
Laos, statistics 66
latitude *29*
Laurasia 9
lava 8
laws 24–25, *24–25*
Lebanon 43
  statistics 66
Leeward Islands 39
Lena, River 42, 90
Lesotho, statistics 63
Lesser Antilles 39
Liberia, statistics 63
Libya, statistics 63
Liechtenstein, statistics 69
limestone cave *9*
lions *35*
Livingstone, David 30
London 54
longitude *29*
Los Angeles 38
Luxembourg, statistics 69
lymph system *42–43*

M
Macao, statistics 67
Mackenzie, Sir Alexander *84*
Madagascar, statistics 63
magma 8
Magna Carta *24*
Malawi, statistics 63

Malaya 26
Malaysia, statistics 67
Maldives, statistics 67
Mali, statistics 63
Malta, statistics 69
mantle (of Earth) 8
Maoris 48, 50, *50*
Mariana Islands 48
Mariana Trench 10
Marshall Islands 48
Martinique, statistics 72
Masai shield 30
Mauritania, statistics 64
Mauritius, statistics 64
Mayotte, statistics 64
Mediterranean Sea 15, 52
Mekong, River 42
Melanesia 48
Melbourne 50
Mexico *15*, 39
  statistics 72
  trade 26
Micronesia 48
Midnight Sun *60*
Milan 58
mission station *33*
Mississippi, River 36
Missouri, River 36
Monaco, statistics 69
monarchy 24
Mongolia 42
  statistics 67
Mongoloids 18–19
monsoon 14, 42
Monserrat, statistics 72
Morocco, statistics 64
Moscow 54, *55*
Mount Cook 48, *50*
Mount Elbruz 53
mountains, table of 90
Mozambique, statistics 64
Muslims 31
Myanmar (Burma)
  statistics 67

N
Namibia, statistics 64
Nauru, statistics 75
Negroids 18–19
Nepal, statistics 67
Netherlands 54, 58
  statistics 69
Netherlands Antilles, statistics 72
New York City *36*, 38
New Zealand 48, *50*
  farming 50
  statistics 75
Niger, statistics 64
Niger, River 30
Nigeria 31–32
  statistics 64
nightjar *59*
Nile, River 30–31
Niue, statistics 75
nomads 43
Norfolk Island, statistics 75
North American 19, 36–38
  climate 36
  map 37
  population growth 19
North Atlantic Drift 11, 52
Norway, statistics 69

Nyasa, Lake 30

O
Ob, River 42
oceans 10–11, *10–11*
  currents 11, *11*
  floors 8
  table of 90
oil 27, 34
  refinery 27, *38*
  Olympic Games 22, 23
  Oman, statistics 67
  Orinoco River 41
  ostrich *34*
  otter *59*

P
Pacific Islands 48
Pacific Islands Trust Territory
  statistics 75
Pacific Ocean 10
Pakistan
  population 46
  statistics 67
pampas 41
Panama 39
  statistics 72
Panama, Isthmus of 72
Pangaea 8–9
Papua New Guinea 48
  statistics 75
Paraguay, statistics 74
Paris 54
penguins *60*
peoples 18–19, *18–19*
Peru 26, 74
  statistics 74
  trade 26
Philippines 47
  statistics 67
picture writing *41*
Pisa, Leaning Tower of 54
Pitcairn Islands, statistics 75
Plate, River 41
plover *35*
Poland, statistics 69
polar bear *60*
Poles, North and South 12, 15
Polynesia 48, *48*
population 18–19
Portugal, statistics 70
Prague 55
prairies 15
Puerto Rico 39
  statistics 72
Puerto Rico Trench 10
Pygmies 32
Pyramids *20*
Pyrenees 52

Q
Qatar, statistics 67

R
rabbit *59*
racial groups 18–19, *18–19*
rain forests 14, *15*, 16–17
  South America 41

rainfall 12, 14
  map *12*
reindeer 59
religions 20–21, *20–21*
republics 25
Reunion, statistics 64
Rhine, River 54
rice growing *46*
Rio de Janeiro *41*
rivers, table of 90
Rocky Mountains 36
Romania, statistics 70
Rome 20, 54
  religion *20*
Rotterdam 57
Russia (and the former Republics of the USSR) 19, 29
  population growth 19
  statistics 70
Russian tsars 81
Rwanda, statistics 64

S
Sahara 30
St Helena, statistics 64
St Kitts-Nevis, statistics 72
St Lucia, statistics 72
St Pierre and Miquelon, statistics 72
St Vincent & the Grenadines, statistics 72
Salween, River 42
Samoa, American, statistics 75
Samoa, Western 48
  statistics 75
San (Bushmen) 32
sand dune *14*
San Francisco, River 41
São Tomé and Principe, statistics 64
Sardinia 56
Saudi Arabia 43
  statistics 67
savanna *14*, 30
Scotland, rulers of 80
sea water, composition 10
seal, crabeater *60*
seasons *15*
Senegal, statistics 64
Seven Wonders of the World 91
Seychelles, statistics 64
Shintoism 21
Shiva 20
shrew *59*
SI units 82
Siberia 42
Sierra Leone, statistics 64
Sikhism 21
silk 26
sill (geology) *8*
Singapore, statistics 67
Sitting Bull *38*
skiing *22*
smallpox 18
snow 15
Solomon Islands 48
  statistics 75
Somali Republic, statistics 64

South Africa 34–35
  statistics 65
  South America 19, 41, *41*
  map *40*
  population growth 19
Soviet Union, the former 42, 53, 55
Spain, statistics 70
species, endangered *16*
Speke, John Hanning *30*
Sphinx *20*
sport 22–23, *22–23*
Sri Lanka, statistics 67
stalagmites and stalagtites *9*
Stanley, Sir Henry Morton *30*
steppes 15, 42
stock exchange 27
Sudan, statistics 65
Sumo wrestling *23*
Surinam, statistics 74
Swaziland, statistics 65
Sweden
  costume *57*
  statistics 70
Switzerland *56*
  statistics 70
Sydney 50
Syria, statistics 67

T

Taiwan

industry 26–27
  statistics 67
Talmud 21
Tanganyika, Lake 30
Tanzania, statistics 65
Taoism 21
Tasmania 50
Tasmanian devil *51*
Technology Revolution 27
Thailand, statistics 67
Tibet 42
tiger *47*
timber 38
time zones *29*
tin 26
Tobago *39*
Togo, statistics 65
Tonga, statistics 75
Torah *21*
trade 26–27, *26–27*
trenches, oceanic 10
Trinidad *39*
Trinidad and Tobago, statistics 73
Tristan da Cunha, statistics 65
tropical forests 30
  North America 36
tropics 30
tundra 15, 42
Tunisia, statistics 65
Turkey 55
  statistics 67

Turks and Caicos Islands, statistics 73
Tuvalu, statistics 75

U

Uganda, statistics 65
Union of Soviet Socialist Republics, statistics 70
  see Soviet Union
United Arab Emirates, statistics 68
United Kingdom
  rulers of 80
  statistics 70
United Nations 16–17, 77–78, *77*
  environmental programme (map) 16–17
  member countries 76, 78
  organization 77
United States of America 26, *36*, 38, 73, 76, 82
  farming 38
  industry 38
  presidents, table of 79
  statistics 73
  trade 26
Ural Mountains 52

uranium 34
Uruguay, statistics 74

V

Vanuatu, statistics 75
Vatican City 55
  statistics 70
vegetation 14–15
Venezuela, statistics 74
Victoria, Lake 30
Vienna 54
Vietnam *47*
  statistics 68
Virgin Islands, statistics 73
Vishnu *20*
volcanic island *8*
volcanoes 8
  cone *8*
Volga, River 54

W

wagon train *38*
Wake Island 48
Wallis and Futuna Islands, statistics 75
wars, table of 76
Washington DC 38
water cycle *13*
waterfalls, table of 90

waves, ocean 11, *11*
weasel *59*
weather 12–13, *12–13*
  forecasting 12
  map 13
Wellington (NZ) 48
West Indies 39, *39*
Western Sahara, statistics 65
wildebeests 34
wind 12
Windward Islands 39
wine-making *54*
World War II 55

Y

Yemen, statistics 68
Yugoslavia, statistics 70

Z

Zaire, statistics 65
Zaire, River 30
Zambesia, River 30
Zambia, statistics 65
zebras 34
Zimbabwe 34
  statistics 65
Zoroastrianism 21

ACKNOWLEDGEMENTS

The publishers wish to thank the following for supplying photographs for this book:

Page 7 Mary Evans Picture Library (middle) ZEFA (bottom); 12 NASA; 14 ZEFA (top) R.I. Lewis (middle) Satour (bottom); 15 ZEFA (top) U.S. Travel (bottom); 16 Bruce Coleman; 20 ZEFA; 21 ZEFA (top) Sonia Halliday Photographs (bottom); 22 Supersport Photos; 23 ZEFA; 24 Popperfoto (top) Mary Evans Picture Library (bottom); 25 ZEFA; 26 Mary Evans Picture Library; 27 ZEFA (top) Vision International (bottom); 30 Mary Evans Picture Library; 32 British Red Cross (top) ZEFA (bottom); 33 Mary Evans Picture Library; 34 ZEFA; 35 Zimbabwe Tourist Office, 36 ZEFA; 38 ZEFA; 39 Trinidad Tourist Board; 41 ZEFA; 42 ZEFA; 43 India Tourist Office; 47 ZEFA; 49 ZEFA; 50 ZEFA; 51 Louise Wright (top) ZEFA (middle); 52 Camera Press; 54 ZEFA; 55 ZEFA; 56 B.J. Cruikshank (left) Swiss National Tourist Office (right); 58 Dennis Gilbert (top) Bart Hofteester (bottom); 61 Vidocq Photo Library; 77 United Nations; 84 The Mansell Collection; 90 U.S. Travel.

Illustrators include: Graham Allen, Sue Barclay, Peter Bull, Jim Channel, Peter Chesterton, Gill Elsbury, John Francis, Jeremy Gower, Chris Lyon, Janos Marffy and Malcolm Porter.